RESTORATIVE SELF-CARE
Planning Journal

A THREE-MONTH DAILY GUIDE

melissa mendez

UNITED HOUSE

Restorative Self-Care Planning Journal—Copyright ©2022 by Melissa Mendez

Published by UNITED HOUSE Publishing

All rights reserved. No portion of this book may be reproduced or shared in any form–electronic, printed, photocopied, recording, or by any information storage and retrieval system, without prior written permission from the publisher. The use of short quotations is permitted.

ISBN: 978-1-952840-29-6

UNITED HOUSE Publishing
Waterford, Michigan

info@unitedhousepublishing.com
www.unitedhousepublishing.com

Cover and interior formatting: Jennifer Johnson. United House Publishing

Published in Waterford, MI
Printed in the United States

2022—First Edition

SPECIAL SALES

Most UNITED HOUSE books are available at special quantity discounts when purchased in bulk by corporations, organizations, and special-interest groups. For information, please e-mail orders@unitedhousepublishing.com

DEAR ROYAL BEAUTY,

Are you ready to create a lifestyle with a simplified flow so you can live abundantly? Maybe you have already tried a variety of planners, journals, hacks, and other tools without success. This journal/planner is different and will simplify your life because it invites you to partner with God. These daily entries allow you to reconnect to your mind, body, and soul and discover how to reign with authority in Christ. Use this as a guide, not another item to add to your checklist.

God created you with purpose on purpose.
You are beautiful and capable.

Your Heavenly Father is waiting for you to **ARISE** and **GLOW** as you are fully **EMBRACING ROYAL BEAUTY.**

Watch our intro video to get started!
Scan QR Code on back cover.

THANK YOU!

melissa mendez

FOUNDER OF
EMBRACING ROYAL BEAUTY
FOLLOW US ON IG

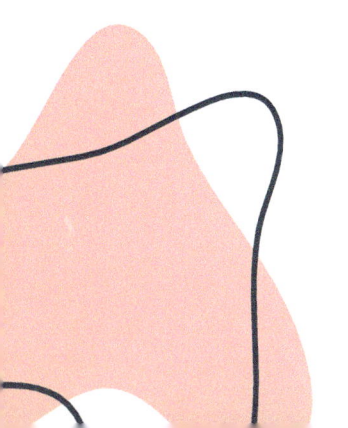

Monthly PLANNER

MONTH OF _____

SUNDAY	MONDAY	TUESDAY	WEDNESDAY	THURSDAY	FRIDAY	SATURDAY

GOALS:

CYCLE TRACKING:

TIPS & TRICKS:
- The best time for a facial is during the follicular phase of your cycle
- Add a simple daily routine of cleansing, toning, hydrating, and protecting your skin
- Enjoy a hydrating mask during the luteal phase of your cycle

Daily PLANNER

DATE:

S M T W T F S

GOD, WHAT ARE TODAY'S PRIORITIES?

- _____
- _____
- _____
- _____
- _____
- _____
- _____
- _____

GOD, WHO DO YOU SAY I AM?

VERSE OF THE WEEK:

MEETINGS:

- _____
- _____
- _____
- _____
- _____

TODAY I AM GRATEFUL FOR:

Daily PRAYER & RECONNECTION

DATE:

S M T W T F S

TODAY I FEEL

WHAT/WHO ARE YOU PRAYING FOR?

- _____
- _____
- _____
- _____

WHAT IS GOD SAYING?

WHAT IS MY ACTION STEP?

MY DECLARATIONS FOR TODAY:

- _____
- _____
- _____
- _____

ACTIVATE & DESCRIBE YOUR SENSES

WHAT THOUGHTS ARE COMING TO ME?

DATE:

S M T W T F S

Daily QUESTIONS & REFLECTIONS

HOW DOES GOD SPEAK TO ME?

WHAT IS GOD SAYING?

GOD, WHO AM I?

Daily PLANNER

DATE:

S M T W T F S

GOD, WHAT ARE TODAY'S PRIORITIES?

○ _____
○ _____
○ _____
○ _____
○ _____
○ _____
○ _____

GOD, WHO DO YOU SAY I AM?

VERSE OF THE WEEK:

MEETINGS:

○ _____
○ _____
○ _____
○ _____
○ _____

TODAY I AM GRATEFUL FOR:

Daily Prayer & Reconnection

DATE:

S M T W T F S

TODAY I FEEL

WHAT/WHO ARE YOU PRAYING FOR?

- _____
- _____
- _____
- _____

WHAT IS MY ACTION STEP?

WHAT IS GOD SAYING?

MY DECLARATIONS FOR TODAY:

- _____
- _____
- _____
- _____

ACTIVATE & DESCRIBE YOUR SENSES

WHAT THOUGHTS ARE COMING TO ME?

DATE:

S M T W T F S

Daily Questions & Reflections

HOW DOES GOD SPEAK TO ME?

WHAT IS GOD SAYING?

GOD, WHO AM I?

Daily PLANNER

DATE:

S M T W T F S

GOD, WHAT ARE TODAY'S PRIORITIES?

- _____
- _____
- _____
- _____
- _____
- _____
- _____

GOD, WHO DO YOU SAY I AM?

VERSE OF THE WEEK:

MEETINGS:

- _____
- _____
- _____
- _____
- _____

TODAY I AM GRATEFUL FOR:

Daily Prayer & Reconnection

DATE:

S M T W T F S

TODAY I FEEL

WHAT/WHO ARE YOU PRAYING FOR?

○ _____
○ _____
○ _____
○ _____

WHAT IS MY ACTION STEP?

WHAT IS GOD SAYING?

MY DECLARATIONS FOR TODAY:

○ _____
○ _____
○ _____
○ _____

ACTIVATE & DESCRIBE YOUR SENSES

WHAT THOUGHTS ARE COMING TO ME?

DATE:

S M T W T F S

Daily QUESTIONS & REFLECTIONS

HOW DOES GOD SPEAK TO ME?

WHAT IS GOD SAYING?

GOD, WHO AM I?

Daily PLANNER

DATE:

S M T W T F S

GOD, WHAT ARE TODAY'S PRIORITIES?

- _____
- _____
- _____
- _____
- _____
- _____
- _____

GOD, WHO DO YOU SAY I AM?

VERSE OF THE WEEK:

MEETINGS:

- _____
- _____
- _____
- _____
- _____

TODAY I AM GRATEFUL FOR:

Daily Prayer & Reconnection

DATE:

S M T W T F S

TODAY I FEEL

WHAT/WHO ARE YOU PRAYING FOR?

○ _____
○ _____
○ _____
○ _____

WHAT IS MY ACTION STEP?

WHAT IS GOD SAYING?

MY DECLARATIONS FOR TODAY:

○ _____
○ _____
○ _____
○ _____

ACTIVATE & DESCRIBE YOUR SENSES

WHAT THOUGHTS ARE COMING TO ME?

DATE:

S M T W T F S

Daily Questions & Reflections

HOW DOES GOD SPEAK TO ME?

WHAT IS GOD SAYING?

GOD, WHO AM I?

Daily PLANNER

DATE:

S M T W T F S

GOD, WHAT ARE TODAY'S PRIORITIES?

○ _____
○ _____
○ _____
○ _____
○ _____
○ _____
○ _____

GOD, WHO DO YOU SAY I AM?

VERSE OF THE WEEK:

MEETINGS:

○ _____
○ _____
○ _____
○ _____
○ _____

TODAY I AM GRATEFUL FOR:

Daily PRAYER & RECONNECTION

DATE:

S M T W T F S

TODAY I FEEL

😊 🙂 😐 🙁 😢

WHAT/WHO ARE YOU PRAYING FOR?

○ _____
○ _____
○ _____
○ _____

WHAT IS MY ACTION STEP?

WHAT IS GOD SAYING?

MY DECLARATIONS FOR TODAY:

○ _____
○ _____
○ _____
○ _____

ACTIVATE & DESCRIBE YOUR SENSES

WHAT THOUGHTS ARE COMING TO ME?

DATE:

S M T W T F S

Daily QUESTIONS & REFLECTIONS

HOW DOES GOD SPEAK TO ME?

WHAT IS GOD SAYING?

GOD, WHO AM I?

Daily PLANNER

DATE:

S M T W T F S

GOD, WHAT ARE TODAY'S PRIORITIES?

○ _____
○ _____
○ _____
○ _____
○ _____
○ _____
○ _____

GOD, WHO DO YOU SAY I AM?

VERSE OF THE WEEK:

MEETINGS:

○ _____
○ _____
○ _____
○ _____
○ _____

TODAY I AM GRATEFUL FOR:

Daily PRAYER & RECONNECTION

DATE:

S M T W T F S

TODAY I FEEL

WHAT/WHO ARE YOU PRAYING FOR?

- _____
- _____
- _____
- _____

WHAT IS MY ACTION STEP?

WHAT IS GOD SAYING?

MY DECLARATIONS FOR TODAY:

- _____
- _____
- _____
- _____

ACTIVATE & DESCRIBE YOUR SENSES

WHAT THOUGHTS ARE COMING TO ME?

DATE:

S M T W T F S

Daily QUESTIONS & REFLECTIONS

HOW DOES GOD SPEAK TO ME?

WHAT IS GOD SAYING?

GOD, WHO AM I?

Daily PLANNER

DATE:

S M T W T F S

GOD, WHAT ARE TODAY'S PRIORITIES?

- _____
- _____
- _____
- _____
- _____
- _____
- _____

GOD, WHO DO YOU SAY I AM?

VERSE OF THE WEEK:

MEETINGS:

- _____
- _____
- _____
- _____
- _____

TODAY I AM GRATEFUL FOR:

Daily PRAYER & RECONNECTION

DATE:

S M T W T F S

TODAY I FEEL
😊 🙂 😐 🙁 😢

WHAT/WHO ARE YOU PRAYING FOR?
○ _____
○ _____
○ _____
○ _____

WHAT IS MY ACTION STEP?

WHAT IS GOD SAYING?

MY DECLARATIONS FOR TODAY:
○ _____
○ _____
○ _____
○ _____

ACTIVATE & DESCRIBE YOUR SENSES

WHAT THOUGHTS ARE COMING TO ME?

DATE:

S M T W T F S

Daily QUESTIONS & REFLECTIONS

HOW DOES GOD SPEAK TO ME?

WHAT IS GOD SAYING?

GOD, WHO AM I?

Daily PLANNER

DATE:

S M T W T F S

GOD, WHAT ARE TODAY'S PRIORITIES?

○ _____
○ _____
○ _____
○ _____
○ _____
○ _____
○ _____

GOD, WHO DO YOU SAY I AM?

VERSE OF THE WEEK:

MEETINGS:

○ _____
○ _____
○ _____
○ _____
○ _____

TODAY I AM GRATEFUL FOR:

Daily Prayer & Reconnection

DATE:

S M T W T F S

TODAY I FEEL

WHAT/WHO ARE YOU PRAYING FOR?

- _____
- _____
- _____
- _____

WHAT IS GOD SAYING?

WHAT IS MY ACTION STEP?

MY DECLARATIONS FOR TODAY:

- _____
- _____
- _____
- _____

ACTIVATE & DESCRIBE YOUR SENSES

WHAT THOUGHTS ARE COMING TO ME?

DATE:

S M T W T F S

Daily QUESTIONS & REFLECTIONS

HOW DOES GOD SPEAK TO ME?

WHAT IS GOD SAYING?

GOD, WHO AM I?

Daily PLANNER

DATE:

S M T W T F S

GOD, WHAT ARE TODAY'S PRIORITIES?

○ _____
○ _____
○ _____
○ _____
○ _____
○ _____
○ _____

GOD, WHO DO YOU SAY I AM?

VERSE OF THE WEEK:

MEETINGS:

○ _____
○ _____
○ _____
○ _____
○ _____

TODAY I AM GRATEFUL FOR:

Daily PRAYER & RECONNECTION

DATE:

S M T W T F S

TODAY I FEEL

WHAT/WHO ARE YOU PRAYING FOR?

- _____
- _____
- _____
- _____

WHAT IS MY ACTION STEP?

WHAT IS GOD SAYING?

MY DECLARATIONS FOR TODAY:

- _____
- _____
- _____
- _____

ACTIVATE & DESCRIBE YOUR SENSES

WHAT THOUGHTS ARE COMING TO ME?

DATE:

S M T W T F S

Daily QUESTIONS & REFLECTIONS

HOW DOES GOD SPEAK TO ME?

WHAT IS GOD SAYING?

GOD, WHO AM I?

Daily PLANNER

DATE:

S M T W T F S

GOD, WHAT ARE TODAY'S PRIORITIES?

- _____
- _____
- _____
- _____
- _____
- _____
- _____

GOD, WHO DO YOU SAY I AM?

VERSE OF THE WEEK:

MEETINGS:

- _____
- _____
- _____
- _____
- _____

TODAY I AM GRATEFUL FOR:

Daily Prayer & Reconnection

DATE:

S M T W T F S

TODAY I FEEL

WHAT/WHO ARE YOU PRAYING FOR?
- _____
- _____
- _____
- _____

WHAT IS MY ACTION STEP?

WHAT IS GOD SAYING?

MY DECLARATIONS FOR TODAY:
- _____
- _____
- _____
- _____

ACTIVATE & DESCRIBE YOUR SENSES

WHAT THOUGHTS ARE COMING TO ME?

DATE:

S M T W T F S

Daily QUESTIONS & REFLECTIONS

HOW DOES GOD SPEAK TO ME?

WHAT IS GOD SAYING?

GOD, WHO AM I?

Daily PLANNER

DATE:

S M T W T F S

GOD, WHAT ARE TODAY'S PRIORITIES?

- ○ _____
- ○ _____
- ○ _____
- ○ _____
- ○ _____
- ○ _____
- ○ _____

GOD, WHO DO YOU SAY I AM?

VERSE OF THE WEEK:

MEETINGS:

- ○ _____
- ○ _____
- ○ _____
- ○ _____
- ○ _____

TODAY I AM GRATEFUL FOR:

Daily Prayer & Reconnection

DATE:

S M T W T F S

TODAY I FEEL

☺ ☺ 😐 ☹ ☹

WHAT/WHO ARE YOU PRAYING FOR?

- _____
- _____
- _____
- _____

WHAT IS MY ACTION STEP?

WHAT IS GOD SAYING?

MY DECLARATIONS FOR TODAY:

- _____
- _____
- _____
- _____

ACTIVATE & DESCRIBE YOUR SENSES

WHAT THOUGHTS ARE COMING TO ME?

DATE:

S M T W T F S

Daily QUESTIONS & REFLECTIONS

HOW DOES GOD SPEAK TO ME?

WHAT IS GOD SAYING?

GOD, WHO AM I?

Daily PLANNER

DATE:

S M T W T F S

GOD, WHAT ARE TODAY'S PRIORITIES?

○ _____
○ _____
○ _____
○ _____
○ _____
○ _____
○ _____

GOD, WHO DO YOU SAY I AM?

VERSE OF THE WEEK:

MEETINGS:

○ _____
○ _____
○ _____
○ _____
○ _____

TODAY I AM GRATEFUL FOR:

Daily Prayer & Reconnection

DATE:

S M T W T F S

TODAY I FEEL

WHAT/WHO ARE YOU PRAYING FOR?

- _____
- _____
- _____
- _____

WHAT IS GOD SAYING?

WHAT IS MY ACTION STEP?

MY DECLARATIONS FOR TODAY:

- _____
- _____
- _____
- _____

ACTIVATE & DESCRIBE YOUR SENSES

WHAT THOUGHTS ARE COMING TO ME?

DATE:

S M T W T F S

Daily Questions & Reflections

HOW DOES GOD SPEAK TO ME?

WHAT IS GOD SAYING?

GOD, WHO AM I?

Daily PLANNER

DATE:

S M T W T F S

GOD, WHAT ARE TODAY'S PRIORITIES?
- _____
- _____
- _____
- _____
- _____
- _____
- _____

GOD, WHO DO YOU SAY I AM?

VERSE OF THE WEEK:

MEETINGS:
- _____
- _____
- _____
- _____
- _____

TODAY I AM GRATEFUL FOR:

Daily Prayer & Reconnection

DATE:

S M T W T F S

TODAY I FEEL

WHAT/WHO ARE YOU PRAYING FOR?

○ _____
○ _____
○ _____
○ _____

WHAT IS MY ACTION STEP?

WHAT IS GOD SAYING?

MY DECLARATIONS FOR TODAY:

○ _____
○ _____
○ _____
○ _____

ACTIVATE & DESCRIBE YOUR SENSES

WHAT THOUGHTS ARE COMING TO ME?

DATE:

S M T W T F S

Daily QUESTIONS & REFLECTIONS

HOW DOES GOD SPEAK TO ME?

WHAT IS GOD SAYING?

GOD, WHO AM I?

Daily PLANNER

DATE:

S M T W T F S

GOD, WHAT ARE TODAY'S PRIORITIES?

- _____
- _____
- _____
- _____
- _____
- _____
- _____

GOD, WHO DO YOU SAY I AM?

VERSE OF THE WEEK:

MEETINGS:

- _____
- _____
- _____
- _____
- _____

TODAY I AM GRATEFUL FOR:

Daily PRAYER & RECONNECTION

DATE:

S M T W T F S

TODAY I FEEL

WHAT/WHO ARE YOU PRAYING FOR?

- _____
- _____
- _____
- _____

WHAT IS GOD SAYING?

WHAT IS MY ACTION STEP?

MY DECLARATIONS FOR TODAY:

- _____
- _____
- _____
- _____

ACTIVATE & DESCRIBE YOUR SENSES

WHAT THOUGHTS ARE COMING TO ME?

DATE:

S M T W T F S

Daily QUESTIONS & REFLECTIONS

HOW DOES GOD SPEAK TO ME?

WHAT IS GOD SAYING?

GOD, WHO AM I?

Daily PLANNER

DATE:

S M T W T F S

GOD, WHAT ARE TODAY'S PRIORITIES?

- _____
- _____
- _____
- _____
- _____
- _____
- _____

GOD, WHO DO YOU SAY I AM?

VERSE OF THE WEEK:

MEETINGS:

- _____
- _____
- _____
- _____
- _____

TODAY I AM GRATEFUL FOR:

Daily PRAYER & RECONNECTION

DATE:

S M T W T F S

TODAY I FEEL

WHAT/WHO ARE YOU PRAYING FOR?

○ _____
○ _____
○ _____
○ _____

WHAT IS GOD SAYING?

WHAT IS MY ACTION STEP?

MY DECLARATIONS FOR TODAY:

○ _____
○ _____
○ _____
○ _____

ACTIVATE & DESCRIBE YOUR SENSES

WHAT THOUGHTS ARE COMING TO ME?

DATE:

S M T W T F S

Daily QUESTIONS & REFLECTIONS

HOW DOES GOD SPEAK TO ME?

WHAT IS GOD SAYING?

GOD, WHO AM I?

Daily PLANNER

DATE:

S M T W T F S

GOD, WHAT ARE TODAY'S PRIORITIES?

○ _____
○ _____
○ _____
○ _____
○ _____
○ _____
○ _____

GOD, WHO DO YOU SAY I AM?

VERSE OF THE WEEK:

MEETINGS:

○ _____
○ _____
○ _____
○ _____
○ _____

TODAY I AM GRATEFUL FOR:

Daily Prayer & Reconnection

DATE:

S M T W T F S

TODAY I FEEL

WHAT/WHO ARE YOU PRAYING FOR?

- _____
- _____
- _____
- _____

WHAT IS MY ACTION STEP?

WHAT IS GOD SAYING?

MY DECLARATIONS FOR TODAY:

- _____
- _____
- _____
- _____

ACTIVATE & DESCRIBE YOUR SENSES

WHAT THOUGHTS ARE COMING TO ME?

DATE:

S M T W T F S

Daily Questions & Reflections

HOW DOES GOD SPEAK TO ME?

WHAT IS GOD SAYING?

GOD, WHO AM I?

Daily PLANNER

DATE:

S M T W T F S

GOD, WHAT ARE TODAY'S PRIORITIES?

- _____
- _____
- _____
- _____
- _____
- _____
- _____

GOD, WHO DO YOU SAY I AM?

VERSE OF THE WEEK:

MEETINGS:

- _____
- _____
- _____
- _____
- _____

TODAY I AM GRATEFUL FOR:

Daily PRAYER & RECONNECTION

DATE:

S M T W T F S

TODAY I FEEL

☺ ☺ 😐 ☹ 😢

WHAT/WHO ARE YOU PRAYING FOR?

○ _____
○ _____
○ _____
○ _____

WHAT IS MY ACTION STEP?

WHAT IS GOD SAYING?

MY DECLARATIONS FOR TODAY:

○ _____
○ _____
○ _____
○ _____

ACTIVATE & DESCRIBE YOUR SENSES

WHAT THOUGHTS ARE COMING TO ME?

DATE:

S M T W T F S

Daily Questions & Reflections

HOW DOES GOD SPEAK TO ME?

WHAT IS GOD SAYING?

GOD, WHO AM I?

Daily PLANNER

DATE:

S M T W T F S

GOD, WHAT ARE TODAY'S PRIORITIES?

○ _____
○ _____
○ _____
○ _____
○ _____
○ _____
○ _____

GOD, WHO DO YOU SAY I AM?

VERSE OF THE WEEK:

MEETINGS:

○ _____
○ _____
○ _____
○ _____
○ _____

TODAY I AM GRATEFUL FOR:

Daily Prayer & Reconnection

DATE:

S M T W T F S

TODAY I FEEL

WHAT/WHO ARE YOU PRAYING FOR?
- _____
- _____
- _____
- _____

WHAT IS MY ACTION STEP?

WHAT IS GOD SAYING?

MY DECLARATIONS FOR TODAY:
- _____
- _____
- _____
- _____

ACTIVATE & DESCRIBE YOUR SENSES

WHAT THOUGHTS ARE COMING TO ME?

DATE:

S M T W T F S

Daily QUESTIONS & REFLECTIONS

HOW DOES GOD SPEAK TO ME?

WHAT IS GOD SAYING?

GOD, WHO AM I?

Daily PLANNER

DATE:

S M T W T F S

GOD, WHAT ARE TODAY'S PRIORITIES?
- ○ _____
- ○ _____
- ○ _____
- ○ _____
- ○ _____
- ○ _____
- ○ _____

GOD, WHO DO YOU SAY I AM?

VERSE OF THE WEEK:

MEETINGS:
- ○ _____
- ○ _____
- ○ _____
- ○ _____
- ○ _____

TODAY I AM GRATEFUL FOR:

Daily PRAYER & RECONNECTION

DATE:

S M T W T F S

TODAY I FEEL

WHAT/WHO ARE YOU PRAYING FOR?

○ _____
○ _____
○ _____
○ _____

WHAT IS MY ACTION STEP?

WHAT IS GOD SAYING?

MY DECLARATIONS FOR TODAY:

○ _____
○ _____
○ _____
○ _____

ACTIVATE & DESCRIBE YOUR SENSES

WHAT THOUGHTS ARE COMING TO ME?

DATE:

S M T W T F S

Daily QUESTIONS & REFLECTIONS

HOW DOES GOD SPEAK TO ME?

WHAT IS GOD SAYING?

GOD, WHO AM I?

Daily PLANNER

DATE:

S M T W T F S

GOD, WHAT ARE TODAY'S PRIORITIES?

○ _____
○ _____
○ _____
○ _____
○ _____
○ _____
○ _____

GOD, WHO DO YOU SAY I AM?

VERSE OF THE WEEK:

MEETINGS:

○ _____
○ _____
○ _____
○ _____
○ _____

TODAY I AM GRATEFUL FOR:

Daily Prayer & Reconnection

DATE:

S M T W T F S

TODAY I FEEL

WHAT/WHO ARE YOU PRAYING FOR?
- _____
- _____
- _____
- _____

WHAT IS MY ACTION STEP?

WHAT IS GOD SAYING?

MY DECLARATIONS FOR TODAY:
- _____
- _____
- _____
- _____

ACTIVATE & DESCRIBE YOUR SENSES

WHAT THOUGHTS ARE COMING TO ME?

DATE:

S M T W T F S

Daily Questions & Reflections

HOW DOES GOD SPEAK TO ME?

WHAT IS GOD SAYING?

GOD, WHO AM I?

Daily PLANNER

DATE:

S M T W T F S

GOD, WHAT ARE TODAY'S PRIORITIES?

- _____
- _____
- _____
- _____
- _____
- _____
- _____

GOD, WHO DO YOU SAY I AM?

VERSE OF THE WEEK:

MEETINGS:

- _____
- _____
- _____
- _____
- _____

TODAY I AM GRATEFUL FOR:

Daily Prayer & Reconnection

DATE:

S M T W T F S

TODAY I FEEL

WHAT/WHO ARE YOU PRAYING FOR?

- ○ _____
- ○ _____
- ○ _____
- ○ _____

WHAT IS MY ACTION STEP?

WHAT IS GOD SAYING?

MY DECLARATIONS FOR TODAY:

- ○ _____
- ○ _____
- ○ _____
- ○ _____

ACTIVATE & DESCRIBE YOUR SENSES

WHAT THOUGHTS ARE COMING TO ME?

DATE:

S M T W T F S

Daily QUESTIONS & REFLECTIONS

HOW DOES GOD SPEAK TO ME?

WHAT IS GOD SAYING?

GOD, WHO AM I?

Daily PLANNER

DATE:

S M T W T F S

GOD, WHAT ARE TODAY'S PRIORITIES?

○ _____
○ _____
○ _____
○ _____
○ _____
○ _____
○ _____

GOD, WHO DO YOU SAY I AM?

VERSE OF THE WEEK:

MEETINGS:

○ _____
○ _____
○ _____
○ _____
○ _____

TODAY I AM GRATEFUL FOR:

Daily Prayer & Reconnection

DATE:

S M T W T F S

TODAY I FEEL

WHAT/WHO ARE YOU PRAYING FOR?
- _____
- _____
- _____
- _____

WHAT IS GOD SAYING?

WHAT IS MY ACTION STEP?

MY DECLARATIONS FOR TODAY:
- _____
- _____
- _____
- _____

ACTIVATE & DESCRIBE YOUR SENSES

WHAT THOUGHTS ARE COMING TO ME?

DATE:

S M T W T F S

Daily QUESTIONS & REFLECTIONS

HOW DOES GOD SPEAK TO ME?

WHAT IS GOD SAYING?

GOD, WHO AM I?

Daily PLANNER

DATE:

S M T W T F S

GOD, WHAT ARE TODAY'S PRIORITIES?

○ _____
○ _____
○ _____
○ _____
○ _____
○ _____
○ _____

GOD, WHO DO YOU SAY I AM?

VERSE OF THE WEEK:

MEETINGS:

○ _____
○ _____
○ _____
○ _____
○ _____

TODAY I AM GRATEFUL FOR:

Daily Prayer & Reconnection

DATE:

S M T W T F S

TODAY I FEEL

WHAT/WHO ARE YOU PRAYING FOR?

○ _____
○ _____
○ _____
○ _____

WHAT IS MY ACTION STEP?

WHAT IS GOD SAYING?

MY DECLARATIONS FOR TODAY:

○ _____
○ _____
○ _____
○ _____

ACTIVATE & DESCRIBE YOUR SENSES

WHAT THOUGHTS ARE COMING TO ME?

DATE:

S M T W T F S

Daily QUESTIONS & REFLECTIONS

HOW DOES GOD SPEAK TO ME?

WHAT IS GOD SAYING?

GOD, WHO AM I?

Daily PLANNER

DATE:

S M T W T F S

GOD, WHAT ARE TODAY'S PRIORITIES?

○ _____
○ _____
○ _____
○ _____
○ _____
○ _____
○ _____

GOD, WHO DO YOU SAY I AM?

VERSE OF THE WEEK:

MEETINGS:

○ _____
○ _____
○ _____
○ _____
○ _____

TODAY I AM GRATEFUL FOR:

Daily Prayer & Reconnection

DATE:

S M T W T F S

TODAY I FEEL

WHAT/WHO ARE YOU PRAYING FOR?

- _____
- _____
- _____
- _____

WHAT IS MY ACTION STEP?

WHAT IS GOD SAYING?

MY DECLARATIONS FOR TODAY:

- _____
- _____
- _____
- _____

ACTIVATE & DESCRIBE YOUR SENSES

WHAT THOUGHTS ARE COMING TO ME?

DATE:

S M T W T F S

Daily Questions & Reflections

HOW DOES GOD SPEAK TO ME?

WHAT IS GOD SAYING?

GOD, WHO AM I?

Daily PLANNER

DATE:

S M T W T F S

GOD, WHAT ARE TODAY'S PRIORITIES?
- ○ _____
- ○ _____
- ○ _____
- ○ _____
- ○ _____
- ○ _____
- ○ _____

GOD, WHO DO YOU SAY I AM?

VERSE OF THE WEEK:

MEETINGS:
- ○ _____
- ○ _____
- ○ _____
- ○ _____
- ○ _____

TODAY I AM GRATEFUL FOR:

Daily PRAYER & RECONNECTION

DATE:

S M T W T F S

TODAY I FEEL

😀 🙂 😐 🙁 😢

WHAT/WHO ARE YOU PRAYING FOR?

- _____
- _____
- _____
- _____

WHAT IS MY ACTION STEP?

WHAT IS GOD SAYING?

MY DECLARATIONS FOR TODAY:

- _____
- _____
- _____
- _____

ACTIVATE & DESCRIBE YOUR SENSES

WHAT THOUGHTS ARE COMING TO ME?

DATE:

S M T W T F S

Daily QUESTIONS & REFLECTIONS

HOW DOES GOD SPEAK TO ME?

WHAT IS GOD SAYING?

GOD, WHO AM I?

Daily PLANNER

DATE:

S M T W T F S

GOD, WHAT ARE TODAY'S PRIORITIES?

○ _____
○ _____
○ _____
○ _____
○ _____
○ _____
○ _____

GOD, WHO DO YOU SAY I AM?

VERSE OF THE WEEK:

MEETINGS:

○ _____
○ _____
○ _____
○ _____
○ _____

TODAY I AM GRATEFUL FOR:

Daily PRAYER & RECONNECTION

DATE:
S M T W T F S

TODAY I FEEL

WHAT/WHO ARE YOU PRAYING FOR?
○ _____
○ _____
○ _____
○ _____

WHAT IS MY ACTION STEP?

WHAT IS GOD SAYING?

MY DECLARATIONS FOR TODAY:
○ _____
○ _____
○ _____
○ _____

ACTIVATE & DESCRIBE YOUR SENSES

WHAT THOUGHTS ARE COMING TO ME?

DATE:

S M T W T F S

Daily Questions & Reflections

HOW DOES GOD SPEAK TO ME?

WHAT IS GOD SAYING?

GOD, WHO AM I?

Daily PLANNER

DATE:

S M T W T F S

GOD, WHAT ARE TODAY'S PRIORITIES?

○ _____
○ _____
○ _____
○ _____
○ _____
○ _____
○ _____

GOD, WHO DO YOU SAY I AM?

VERSE OF THE WEEK:

MEETINGS:

○ _____
○ _____
○ _____
○ _____
○ _____

TODAY I AM GRATEFUL FOR:

Daily Prayer & Reconnection

DATE:

S M T W T F S

TODAY I FEEL

WHAT/WHO ARE YOU PRAYING FOR?

- _____
- _____
- _____
- _____

WHAT IS MY ACTION STEP?

WHAT IS GOD SAYING?

MY DECLARATIONS FOR TODAY:

- _____
- _____
- _____
- _____

ACTIVATE & DESCRIBE YOUR SENSES

WHAT THOUGHTS ARE COMING TO ME?

DATE:

S M T W T F S

Daily QUESTIONS & REFLECTIONS

HOW DOES GOD SPEAK TO ME?

WHAT IS GOD SAYING?

GOD, WHO AM I?

Daily PLANNER

DATE:

S M T W T F S

GOD, WHAT ARE TODAY'S PRIORITIES?

○ _____
○ _____
○ _____
○ _____
○ _____
○ _____
○ _____

GOD, WHO DO YOU SAY I AM?

VERSE OF THE WEEK:

MEETINGS:

○ _____
○ _____
○ _____
○ _____
○ _____

TODAY I AM GRATEFUL FOR:

Daily Prayer & Reconnection

DATE:

S M T W T F S

TODAY I FEEL

WHAT/WHO ARE YOU PRAYING FOR?

- _____
- _____
- _____
- _____

WHAT IS MY ACTION STEP?

WHAT IS GOD SAYING?

MY DECLARATIONS FOR TODAY:

- _____
- _____
- _____
- _____

ACTIVATE & DESCRIBE YOUR SENSES

WHAT THOUGHTS ARE COMING TO ME?

DATE:

S M T W T F S

Daily Questions & Reflections

HOW DOES GOD SPEAK TO ME?

WHAT IS GOD SAYING?

GOD, WHO AM I?

Daily PLANNER

DATE:

S M T W T F S

GOD, WHAT ARE TODAY'S PRIORITIES?

○ _____
○ _____
○ _____
○ _____
○ _____
○ _____
○ _____

GOD, WHO DO YOU SAY I AM?

VERSE OF THE WEEK:

MEETINGS:

○ _____
○ _____
○ _____
○ _____
○ _____

TODAY I AM GRATEFUL FOR:

Daily PRAYER & RECONNECTION

DATE:

S M T W T F S

TODAY I FEEL

😊 🙂 😐 🙁 😢

WHAT/WHO ARE YOU PRAYING FOR?

○ _____
○ _____
○ _____
○ _____

WHAT IS MY ACTION STEP?

WHAT IS GOD SAYING?

MY DECLARATIONS FOR TODAY:

○ _____
○ _____
○ _____
○ _____

ACTIVATE & DESCRIBE YOUR SENSES

WHAT THOUGHTS ARE COMING TO ME?

DATE:

S M T W T F S

Daily Questions & Reflections

HOW DOES GOD SPEAK TO ME?

WHAT IS GOD SAYING?

GOD, WHO AM I?

Daily PLANNER

DATE:

S M T W T F S

GOD, WHAT ARE TODAY'S PRIORITIES?

○ _____
○ _____
○ _____
○ _____
○ _____
○ _____
○ _____

GOD, WHO DO YOU SAY I AM?

VERSE OF THE WEEK:

MEETINGS:

○ _____
○ _____
○ _____
○ _____
○ _____

TODAY I AM GRATEFUL FOR:

Daily PRAYER & RECONNECTION

DATE:

S M T W T F S

TODAY I FEEL

WHAT/WHO ARE YOU PRAYING FOR?

- _____
- _____
- _____
- _____

WHAT IS MY ACTION STEP?

WHAT IS GOD SAYING?

MY DECLARATIONS FOR TODAY:

- _____
- _____
- _____
- _____

ACTIVATE & DESCRIBE YOUR SENSES

WHAT THOUGHTS ARE COMING TO ME?

DATE:

S M T W T F S

Daily QUESTIONS & REFLECTIONS

HOW DOES GOD SPEAK TO ME?

WHAT IS GOD SAYING?

GOD, WHO AM I?

Daily PLANNER

DATE:

S M T W T F S

GOD, WHAT ARE TODAY'S PRIORITIES?
- ○ _____
- ○ _____
- ○ _____
- ○ _____
- ○ _____
- ○ _____
- ○ _____

GOD, WHO DO YOU SAY I AM?

VERSE OF THE WEEK:

MEETINGS:
- ○ _____
- ○ _____
- ○ _____
- ○ _____
- ○ _____

TODAY I AM GRATEFUL FOR:

Daily PRAYER & RECONNECTION

DATE:

S M T W T F S

TODAY I FEEL

WHAT/WHO ARE YOU PRAYING FOR?

○ _____
○ _____
○ _____
○ _____

WHAT IS MY ACTION STEP?

WHAT IS GOD SAYING?

MY DECLARATIONS FOR TODAY:

○ _____
○ _____
○ _____
○ _____

ACTIVATE & DESCRIBE YOUR SENSES

WHAT THOUGHTS ARE COMING TO ME?

DATE:

S M T W T F S

Daily QUESTIONS & REFLECTIONS

HOW DOES GOD SPEAK TO ME?

WHAT IS GOD SAYING?

GOD, WHO AM I?

Monthly PLANNER

MONTH OF _____

SUNDAY	MONDAY	TUESDAY	WEDNESDAY	THURSDAY	FRIDAY	SATURDAY

GOALS:

CYCLE TRACKING:

TIPS & TRICKS:
- The best time for a facial is during the follicular phase of your cycle
- Add a simple daily routine of cleansing, toning, hydrating, and protecting your skin
- Enjoy a hydrating mask during the luteal phase of your cycle

Daily PLANNER

DATE:

S M T W T F S

GOD, WHAT ARE TODAY'S PRIORITIES?

- ☐ _____
- ☐ _____
- ☐ _____
- ☐ _____
- ☐ _____
- ☐ _____
- ☐ _____

GOD, WHO DO YOU SAY I AM?

VERSE OF THE WEEK:

MEETINGS:

- ☐ _____
- ☐ _____
- ☐ _____
- ☐ _____
- ☐ _____

TODAY I AM GRATEFUL FOR:

Daily PRAYER & RECONNECTION

DATE:

S M T W T F S

TODAY I FEEL

☺ ☺ 😐 ☹ ☹

WHAT/WHO ARE YOU PRAYING FOR?

○ _____
○ _____
○ _____
○ _____

WHAT IS MY ACTION STEP?

WHAT IS GOD SAYING?

MY DECLARATIONS FOR TODAY:

○ _____
○ _____
○ _____
○ _____

ACTIVATE & DESCRIBE YOUR SENSES

WHAT THOUGHTS ARE COMING TO ME?

DATE:

S M T W T F S

Daily QUESTIONS & REFLECTIONS

HOW DOES GOD SPEAK TO ME?

WHAT IS GOD SAYING?

GOD, WHO AM I?

Daily PLANNER

DATE:

S M T W T F S

GOD, WHAT ARE TODAY'S PRIORITIES?

○ _____
○ _____
○ _____
○ _____
○ _____
○ _____
○ _____

GOD, WHO DO YOU SAY I AM?

VERSE OF THE WEEK:

MEETINGS:

○ _____
○ _____
○ _____
○ _____
○ _____

TODAY I AM GRATEFUL FOR:

Daily Prayer & Reconnection

DATE:

S M T W T F S

TODAY I FEEL

WHAT/WHO ARE YOU PRAYING FOR?

- _____
- _____
- _____
- _____

WHAT IS GOD SAYING?

WHAT IS MY ACTION STEP?

MY DECLARATIONS FOR TODAY:

- _____
- _____
- _____
- _____

ACTIVATE & DESCRIBE YOUR SENSES

WHAT THOUGHTS ARE COMING TO ME?

DATE:

S M T W T F S

Daily Questions & Reflections

HOW DOES GOD SPEAK TO ME?

WHAT IS GOD SAYING?

GOD, WHO AM I?

Daily PLANNER

DATE:

S M T W T F S

GOD, WHAT ARE TODAY'S PRIORITIES?
- _____
- _____
- _____
- _____
- _____
- _____
- _____

GOD, WHO DO YOU SAY I AM?

VERSE OF THE WEEK:

MEETINGS:
- _____
- _____
- _____
- _____
- _____

TODAY I AM GRATEFUL FOR:

Daily Prayer & Reconnection

DATE:

S M T W T F S

TODAY I FEEL

WHAT/WHO ARE YOU PRAYING FOR?

- _____
- _____
- _____
- _____

WHAT IS MY ACTION STEP?

WHAT IS GOD SAYING?

MY DECLARATIONS FOR TODAY:

- _____
- _____
- _____
- _____

ACTIVATE & DESCRIBE YOUR SENSES

WHAT THOUGHTS ARE COMING TO ME?

DATE:

S M T W T F S

Daily QUESTIONS & REFLECTIONS

HOW DOES GOD SPEAK TO ME?

WHAT IS GOD SAYING?

GOD, WHO AM I?

Daily PLANNER

DATE:

S M T W T F S

GOD, WHAT ARE TODAY'S PRIORITIES?

- _____
- _____
- _____
- _____
- _____
- _____
- _____

GOD, WHO DO YOU SAY I AM?

VERSE OF THE WEEK:

MEETINGS:

- _____
- _____
- _____
- _____
- _____

TODAY I AM GRATEFUL FOR:

Daily Prayer & Reconnection

DATE:

S M T W T F S

TODAY I FEEL

WHAT/WHO ARE YOU PRAYING FOR?

- _____
- _____
- _____
- _____

WHAT IS MY ACTION STEP?

WHAT IS GOD SAYING?

MY DECLARATIONS FOR TODAY:

- _____
- _____
- _____
- _____

ACTIVATE & DESCRIBE YOUR SENSES

WHAT THOUGHTS ARE COMING TO ME?

DATE:

S M T W T F S

Daily QUESTIONS & REFLECTIONS

HOW DOES GOD SPEAK TO ME?

WHAT IS GOD SAYING?

GOD, WHO AM I?

Daily PLANNER

DATE:

S M T W T F S

GOD, WHAT ARE TODAY'S PRIORITIES?

○ _____
○ _____
○ _____
○ _____
○ _____
○ _____
○ _____

GOD, WHO DO YOU SAY I AM?

VERSE OF THE WEEK:

MEETINGS:

○ _____
○ _____
○ _____
○ _____
○ _____

TODAY I AM GRATEFUL FOR:

Daily PRAYER & RECONNECTION

DATE:

S M T W T F S

TODAY I FEEL

WHAT/WHO ARE YOU PRAYING FOR?

○ _____
○ _____
○ _____
○ _____

WHAT IS GOD SAYING?

WHAT IS MY ACTION STEP?

MY DECLARATIONS FOR TODAY:

○ _____
○ _____
○ _____
○ _____

ACTIVATE & DESCRIBE YOUR SENSES

WHAT THOUGHTS ARE COMING TO ME?

DATE:

S M T W T F S

Daily QUESTIONS & REFLECTIONS

HOW DOES GOD SPEAK TO ME?

WHAT IS GOD SAYING?

GOD, WHO AM I?

Daily PLANNER

DATE:

S M T W T F S

GOD, WHAT ARE TODAY'S PRIORITIES?

○ _____
○ _____
○ _____
○ _____
○ _____
○ _____
○ _____

GOD, WHO DO YOU SAY I AM?

VERSE OF THE WEEK:

MEETINGS:

○ _____
○ _____
○ _____
○ _____
○ _____

TODAY I AM GRATEFUL FOR:

Daily PRAYER & RECONNECTION

DATE:
S M T W T F S

TODAY I FEEL

WHAT/WHO ARE YOU PRAYING FOR?

- _____
- _____
- _____
- _____

WHAT IS GOD SAYING?

WHAT IS MY ACTION STEP?

MY DECLARATIONS FOR TODAY:

- _____
- _____
- _____
- _____

ACTIVATE & DESCRIBE YOUR SENSES

WHAT THOUGHTS ARE COMING TO ME?

DATE:

S M T W T F S

Daily QUESTIONS & REFLECTIONS

HOW DOES GOD SPEAK TO ME?

WHAT IS GOD SAYING?

GOD, WHO AM I?

Daily PLANNER

DATE:

S M T W T F S

GOD, WHAT ARE TODAY'S PRIORITIES?

- _____
- _____
- _____
- _____
- _____
- _____
- _____

GOD, WHO DO YOU SAY I AM?

VERSE OF THE WEEK:

MEETINGS:

- _____
- _____
- _____
- _____
- _____

TODAY I AM GRATEFUL FOR:

Daily PRAYER & RECONNECTION

DATE:

S M T W T F S

TODAY I FEEL

😊 🙂 😐 🙁 😢

WHAT/WHO ARE YOU PRAYING FOR?
- _____
- _____
- _____
- _____

WHAT IS MY ACTION STEP?

WHAT IS GOD SAYING?

MY DECLARATIONS FOR TODAY:
- _____
- _____
- _____
- _____

ACTIVATE & DESCRIBE YOUR SENSES

WHAT THOUGHTS ARE COMING TO ME?

DATE:

S M T W T F S

Daily QUESTIONS & REFLECTIONS

HOW DOES GOD SPEAK TO ME?

WHAT IS GOD SAYING?

GOD, WHO AM I?

Daily PLANNER

DATE:

S M T W T F S

GOD, WHAT ARE TODAY'S PRIORITIES?

○ _____
○ _____
○ _____
○ _____
○ _____
○ _____
○ _____

GOD, WHO DO YOU SAY I AM?

VERSE OF THE WEEK:

MEETINGS:

○ _____
○ _____
○ _____
○ _____
○ _____

TODAY I AM GRATEFUL FOR:

Daily PRAYER & RECONNECTION

DATE:

S M T W T F S

TODAY I FEEL

WHAT/WHO ARE YOU PRAYING FOR?
○ _____
○ _____
○ _____
○ _____

WHAT IS GOD SAYING?

WHAT IS MY ACTION STEP?

MY DECLARATIONS FOR TODAY:
○ _____
○ _____
○ _____
○ _____

ACTIVATE & DESCRIBE YOUR SENSES

WHAT THOUGHTS ARE COMING TO ME?

DATE:

S M T W T F S

Daily QUESTIONS & REFLECTIONS

HOW DOES GOD SPEAK TO ME?

WHAT IS GOD SAYING?

GOD, WHO AM I?

Daily PLANNER

DATE:

S M T W T F S

GOD, WHAT ARE TODAY'S PRIORITIES?

- ○ _____
- ○ _____
- ○ _____
- ○ _____
- ○ _____
- ○ _____
- ○ _____

GOD, WHO DO YOU SAY I AM?

VERSE OF THE WEEK:

MEETINGS:

- ○ _____
- ○ _____
- ○ _____
- ○ _____
- ○ _____

TODAY I AM GRATEFUL FOR:

Daily PRAYER & RECONNECTION

DATE:

S M T W T F S

TODAY I FEEL

WHAT/WHO ARE YOU PRAYING FOR?
- _____
- _____
- _____
- _____

WHAT IS GOD SAYING?

WHAT IS MY ACTION STEP?

MY DECLARATIONS FOR TODAY:
- _____
- _____
- _____
- _____

ACTIVATE & DESCRIBE YOUR SENSES

WHAT THOUGHTS ARE COMING TO ME?

DATE:

S M T W T F S

Daily QUESTIONS & REFLECTIONS

HOW DOES GOD SPEAK TO ME?

WHAT IS GOD SAYING?

GOD, WHO AM I?

Daily PLANNER

DATE:

S M T W T F S

GOD, WHAT ARE TODAY'S PRIORITIES?

○ _____
○ _____
○ _____
○ _____
○ _____
○ _____
○ _____

GOD, WHO DO YOU SAY I AM?

VERSE OF THE WEEK:

MEETINGS:

○ _____
○ _____
○ _____
○ _____
○ _____

TODAY I AM GRATEFUL FOR:

Daily Prayer & Reconnection

DATE:

S M T W T F S

TODAY I FEEL

WHAT/WHO ARE YOU PRAYING FOR?

○ _____
○ _____
○ _____
○ _____

WHAT IS MY ACTION STEP?

WHAT IS GOD SAYING?

MY DECLARATIONS FOR TODAY:

○ _____
○ _____
○ _____
○ _____

ACTIVATE & DESCRIBE YOUR SENSES

WHAT THOUGHTS ARE COMING TO ME?

DATE:

S M T W T F S

Daily QUESTIONS & REFLECTIONS

HOW DOES GOD SPEAK TO ME?

WHAT IS GOD SAYING?

GOD, WHO AM I?

Daily PLANNER

DATE:

S M T W T F S

GOD, WHAT ARE TODAY'S PRIORITIES?

○ _____
○ _____
○ _____
○ _____
○ _____
○ _____
○ _____

GOD, WHO DO YOU SAY I AM?

VERSE OF THE WEEK:

MEETINGS:

○ _____
○ _____
○ _____
○ _____
○ _____

TODAY I AM GRATEFUL FOR:

Daily Prayer & Reconnection

DATE:

S M T W T F S

TODAY I FEEL

WHAT/WHO ARE YOU PRAYING FOR?

○ _____
○ _____
○ _____
○ _____

WHAT IS MY ACTION STEP?

WHAT IS GOD SAYING?

MY DECLARATIONS FOR TODAY:

○ _____
○ _____
○ _____
○ _____

ACTIVATE & DESCRIBE YOUR SENSES

WHAT THOUGHTS ARE COMING TO ME?

DATE:

S M T W T F S

Daily QUESTIONS & REFLECTIONS

HOW DOES GOD SPEAK TO ME?

WHAT IS GOD SAYING?

GOD, WHO AM I?

Daily PLANNER

DATE:

S M T W T F S

GOD, WHAT ARE TODAY'S PRIORITIES?

○ _____
○ _____
○ _____
○ _____
○ _____
○ _____
○ _____

GOD, WHO DO YOU SAY I AM?

VERSE OF THE WEEK:

MEETINGS:

○ _____
○ _____
○ _____
○ _____
○ _____

TODAY I AM GRATEFUL FOR:

Daily Prayer & Reconnection

DATE:

S M T W T F S

TODAY I FEEL

WHAT/WHO ARE YOU PRAYING FOR?

○ _____
○ _____
○ _____
○ _____

WHAT IS GOD SAYING?

WHAT IS MY ACTION STEP?

MY DECLARATIONS FOR TODAY:

○ _____
○ _____
○ _____
○ _____

ACTIVATE & DESCRIBE YOUR SENSES

WHAT THOUGHTS ARE COMING TO ME?

DATE:

S M T W T F S

Daily QUESTIONS & REFLECTIONS

HOW DOES GOD SPEAK TO ME?

WHAT IS GOD SAYING?

GOD, WHO AM I?

Daily PLANNER

DATE:

S M T W T F S

GOD, WHAT ARE TODAY'S PRIORITIES?

○ _____
○ _____
○ _____
○ _____
○ _____
○ _____
○ _____

GOD, WHO DO YOU SAY I AM?

VERSE OF THE WEEK:

MEETINGS:

○ _____
○ _____
○ _____
○ _____
○ _____

TODAY I AM GRATEFUL FOR:

Daily PRAYER & RECONNECTION

DATE:

S M T W T F S

TODAY I FEEL

WHAT/WHO ARE YOU PRAYING FOR?

○ _____
○ _____
○ _____
○ _____

WHAT IS MY ACTION STEP?

WHAT IS GOD SAYING?

MY DECLARATIONS FOR TODAY:

○ _____
○ _____
○ _____
○ _____

ACTIVATE & DESCRIBE YOUR SENSES

WHAT THOUGHTS ARE COMING TO ME?

DATE:

S M T W T F S

Daily QUESTIONS & REFLECTIONS

HOW DOES GOD SPEAK TO ME?

WHAT IS GOD SAYING?

GOD, WHO AM I?

Daily PLANNER

DATE:

S M T W T F S

GOD, WHAT ARE TODAY'S PRIORITIES?

○ _____
○ _____
○ _____
○ _____
○ _____
○ _____
○ _____

GOD, WHO DO YOU SAY I AM?

VERSE OF THE WEEK:

MEETINGS:

○ _____
○ _____
○ _____
○ _____
○ _____

TODAY I AM GRATEFUL FOR:

Daily PRAYER & RECONNECTION

DATE:

S M T W T F S

TODAY I FEEL

😊 🙂 😐 🙁 😢

WHAT/WHO ARE YOU PRAYING FOR?

○ _____
○ _____
○ _____
○ _____

WHAT IS MY ACTION STEP?

WHAT IS GOD SAYING?

MY DECLARATIONS FOR TODAY:

○ _____
○ _____
○ _____
○ _____

ACTIVATE & DESCRIBE YOUR SENSES

WHAT THOUGHTS ARE COMING TO ME?

DATE:

S M T W T F S

Daily Questions & Reflections

HOW DOES GOD SPEAK TO ME?

WHAT IS GOD SAYING?

GOD, WHO AM I?

Daily PLANNER

DATE:

S M T W T F S

GOD, WHAT ARE TODAY'S PRIORITIES?
- _____
- _____
- _____
- _____
- _____
- _____
- _____
- _____

GOD, WHO DO YOU SAY I AM?

VERSE OF THE WEEK:

MEETINGS:
- _____
- _____
- _____
- _____
- _____

TODAY I AM GRATEFUL FOR:

Daily Prayer & Reconnection

DATE:

S M T W T F S

TODAY I FEEL

😊 🙂 😐 🙁 😢

WHAT/WHO ARE YOU PRAYING FOR?

○ _____
○ _____
○ _____
○ _____

WHAT IS MY ACTION STEP?

WHAT IS GOD SAYING?

MY DECLARATIONS FOR TODAY:

○ _____
○ _____
○ _____
○ _____

ACTIVATE & DESCRIBE YOUR SENSES

WHAT THOUGHTS ARE COMING TO ME?

DATE:

S M T W T F S

Daily QUESTIONS & REFLECTIONS

HOW DOES GOD SPEAK TO ME?

WHAT IS GOD SAYING?

GOD, WHO AM I?

Daily PLANNER

DATE:

S M T W T F S

GOD, WHAT ARE TODAY'S PRIORITIES?
- _____
- _____
- _____
- _____
- _____
- _____
- _____

GOD, WHO DO YOU SAY I AM?

VERSE OF THE WEEK:

MEETINGS:
- _____
- _____
- _____
- _____
- _____

TODAY I AM GRATEFUL FOR:

Daily PRAYER & RECONNECTION

DATE:

S M T W T F S

TODAY I FEEL

WHAT/WHO ARE YOU PRAYING FOR?

- _____
- _____
- _____
- _____

WHAT IS GOD SAYING?

WHAT IS MY ACTION STEP?

MY DECLARATIONS FOR TODAY:

- _____
- _____
- _____
- _____

ACTIVATE & DESCRIBE YOUR SENSES

WHAT THOUGHTS ARE COMING TO ME?

DATE:

S M T W T F S

Daily Questions & Reflections

HOW DOES GOD SPEAK TO ME?

WHAT IS GOD SAYING?

GOD, WHO AM I?

Daily PLANNER

DATE:

S M T W T F S

GOD, WHAT ARE TODAY'S PRIORITIES?

- _____
- _____
- _____
- _____
- _____
- _____
- _____

GOD, WHO DO YOU SAY I AM?

VERSE OF THE WEEK:

MEETINGS:

- _____
- _____
- _____
- _____
- _____

TODAY I AM GRATEFUL FOR:

Daily Prayer & Reconnection

DATE:

S M T W T F S

TODAY I FEEL

WHAT/WHO ARE YOU PRAYING FOR?

- _____
- _____
- _____
- _____

WHAT IS GOD SAYING?

WHAT IS MY ACTION STEP?

MY DECLARATIONS FOR TODAY:

- _____
- _____
- _____
- _____

ACTIVATE & DESCRIBE YOUR SENSES

WHAT THOUGHTS ARE COMING TO ME?

DATE:

S M T W T F S

Daily QUESTIONS & REFLECTIONS

HOW DOES GOD SPEAK TO ME?

WHAT IS GOD SAYING?

GOD, WHO AM I?

Daily PLANNER

DATE:

S M T W T F S

GOD, WHAT ARE TODAY'S PRIORITIES?

- _____
- _____
- _____
- _____
- _____
- _____
- _____

GOD, WHO DO YOU SAY I AM?

VERSE OF THE WEEK:

MEETINGS:

- _____
- _____
- _____
- _____
- _____

TODAY I AM GRATEFUL FOR:

Daily PRAYER & RECONNECTION

DATE:

S M T W T F S

TODAY I FEEL

WHAT/WHO ARE YOU PRAYING FOR?

○ _____
○ _____
○ _____
○ _____

WHAT IS MY ACTION STEP?

WHAT IS GOD SAYING?

MY DECLARATIONS FOR TODAY:

○ _____
○ _____
○ _____
○ _____

ACTIVATE & DESCRIBE YOUR SENSES

WHAT THOUGHTS ARE COMING TO ME?

DATE:

S M T W T F S

Daily Questions & Reflections

HOW DOES GOD SPEAK TO ME?

WHAT IS GOD SAYING?

GOD, WHO AM I?

Daily PLANNER

DATE:

S M T W T F S

GOD, WHAT ARE TODAY'S PRIORITIES?

○ _____
○ _____
○ _____
○ _____
○ _____
○ _____
○ _____

GOD, WHO DO YOU SAY I AM?

VERSE OF THE WEEK:

MEETINGS:

○ _____
○ _____
○ _____
○ _____
○ _____

TODAY I AM GRATEFUL FOR:

Daily Prayer & Reconnection

DATE:

S M T W T F S

TODAY I FEEL

WHAT/WHO ARE YOU PRAYING FOR?

○ _____
○ _____
○ _____
○ _____

WHAT IS MY ACTION STEP?

WHAT IS GOD SAYING?

MY DECLARATIONS FOR TODAY:

○ _____
○ _____
○ _____
○ _____

ACTIVATE & DESCRIBE YOUR SENSES

WHAT THOUGHTS ARE COMING TO ME?

DATE:

S M T W T F S

Daily QUESTIONS & REFLECTIONS

HOW DOES GOD SPEAK TO ME?

WHAT IS GOD SAYING?

GOD, WHO AM I?

Daily PLANNER

DATE:

S M T W T F S

GOD, WHAT ARE TODAY'S PRIORITIES?

○ _____
○ _____
○ _____
○ _____
○ _____
○ _____
○ _____
○ _____

GOD, WHO DO YOU SAY I AM?

VERSE OF THE WEEK:

MEETINGS:

○ _____
○ _____
○ _____
○ _____
○ _____

TODAY I AM GRATEFUL FOR:

Daily Prayer & Reconnection

DATE:

S M T W T F S

TODAY I FEEL

😃 🙂 😐 🙁 😢

WHAT/WHO ARE YOU PRAYING FOR?
- _____
- _____
- _____
- _____

WHAT IS MY ACTION STEP?

WHAT IS GOD SAYING?

MY DECLARATIONS FOR TODAY:
- _____
- _____
- _____
- _____

ACTIVATE & DESCRIBE YOUR SENSES

WHAT THOUGHTS ARE COMING TO ME?

DATE:

S M T W T F S

Daily Questions & Reflections

HOW DOES GOD SPEAK TO ME?

WHAT IS GOD SAYING?

GOD, WHO AM I?

Daily PLANNER

DATE:

S M T W T F S

GOD, WHAT ARE TODAY'S PRIORITIES?
- ○ _____
- ○ _____
- ○ _____
- ○ _____
- ○ _____
- ○ _____
- ○ _____

GOD, WHO DO YOU SAY I AM?

VERSE OF THE WEEK:

MEETINGS:
- ○ _____
- ○ _____
- ○ _____
- ○ _____
- ○ _____

TODAY I AM GRATEFUL FOR:

Daily PRAYER & RECONNECTION

DATE:

S M T W T F S

TODAY I FEEL

WHAT/WHO ARE YOU PRAYING FOR?

○ _____
○ _____
○ _____
○ _____

WHAT IS GOD SAYING?

WHAT IS MY ACTION STEP?

MY DECLARATIONS FOR TODAY:

○ _____
○ _____
○ _____
○ _____

ACTIVATE & DESCRIBE YOUR SENSES

WHAT THOUGHTS ARE COMING TO ME?

DATE:

S M T W T F S

Daily QUESTIONS & REFLECTIONS

HOW DOES GOD SPEAK TO ME?

WHAT IS GOD SAYING?

GOD, WHO AM I?

Daily PLANNER

DATE:

S M T W T F S

GOD, WHAT ARE TODAY'S PRIORITIES?

- _____
- _____
- _____
- _____
- _____
- _____
- _____

GOD, WHO DO YOU SAY I AM?

VERSE OF THE WEEK:

MEETINGS:

- _____
- _____
- _____
- _____
- _____

TODAY I AM GRATEFUL FOR:

Daily Prayer & Reconnection

DATE:

S M T W T F S

TODAY I FEEL

😊 🙂 😐 🙁 😢

WHAT/WHO ARE YOU PRAYING FOR?

- _____
- _____
- _____
- _____

WHAT IS GOD SAYING?

WHAT IS MY ACTION STEP?

MY DECLARATIONS FOR TODAY:

- _____
- _____
- _____
- _____

ACTIVATE & DESCRIBE YOUR SENSES

WHAT THOUGHTS ARE COMING TO ME?

DATE:

S M T W T F S

Daily QUESTIONS & REFLECTIONS

HOW DOES GOD SPEAK TO ME?

WHAT IS GOD SAYING?

GOD, WHO AM I?

Daily PLANNER

DATE:

S M T W T F S

GOD, WHAT ARE TODAY'S PRIORITIES?
- _____
- _____
- _____
- _____
- _____
- _____
- _____

GOD, WHO DO YOU SAY I AM?

VERSE OF THE WEEK:

MEETINGS:
- _____
- _____
- _____
- _____
- _____

TODAY I AM GRATEFUL FOR:

Daily PRAYER & RECONNECTION

DATE:

S M T W T F S

TODAY I FEEL

WHAT/WHO ARE YOU PRAYING FOR?

○ _____
○ _____
○ _____
○ _____

WHAT IS GOD SAYING?

WHAT IS MY ACTION STEP?

MY DECLARATIONS FOR TODAY:

○ _____
○ _____
○ _____
○ _____

ACTIVATE & DESCRIBE YOUR SENSES

WHAT THOUGHTS ARE COMING TO ME?

DATE:

S M T W T F S

Daily QUESTIONS & REFLECTIONS

HOW DOES GOD SPEAK TO ME?

WHAT IS GOD SAYING?

GOD, WHO AM I?

Daily PLANNER

DATE:

S M T W T F S

GOD, WHAT ARE TODAY'S PRIORITIES?

- _____
- _____
- _____
- _____
- _____
- _____
- _____

GOD, WHO DO YOU SAY I AM?

VERSE OF THE WEEK:

MEETINGS:

- _____
- _____
- _____
- _____
- _____

TODAY I AM GRATEFUL FOR:

Daily PRAYER & RECONNECTION

DATE:

S M T W T F S

TODAY I FEEL

WHAT/WHO ARE YOU PRAYING FOR?

- _____
- _____
- _____
- _____

WHAT IS MY ACTION STEP?

WHAT IS GOD SAYING?

MY DECLARATIONS FOR TODAY:

- _____
- _____
- _____
- _____

ACTIVATE & DESCRIBE YOUR SENSES

WHAT THOUGHTS ARE COMING TO ME?

DATE:

S M T W T F S

Daily Questions & Reflections

HOW DOES GOD SPEAK TO ME?

WHAT IS GOD SAYING?

GOD, WHO AM I?

Daily PLANNER

DATE:

S M T W T F S

GOD, WHAT ARE TODAY'S PRIORITIES?

- _____
- _____
- _____
- _____
- _____
- _____
- _____

GOD, WHO DO YOU SAY I AM?

VERSE OF THE WEEK:

MEETINGS:

- _____
- _____
- _____
- _____
- _____

TODAY I AM GRATEFUL FOR:

Daily PRAYER & RECONNECTION

DATE:

S M T W T F S

TODAY I FEEL

WHAT/WHO ARE YOU PRAYING FOR?

○ _____
○ _____
○ _____
○ _____

WHAT IS GOD SAYING?

WHAT IS MY ACTION STEP?

MY DECLARATIONS FOR TODAY:

○ _____
○ _____
○ _____
○ _____

ACTIVATE & DESCRIBE YOUR SENSES

WHAT THOUGHTS ARE COMING TO ME?

DATE:

S M T W T F S

Daily QUESTIONS & REFLECTIONS

HOW DOES GOD SPEAK TO ME?

WHAT IS GOD SAYING?

GOD, WHO AM I?

Daily PLANNER

DATE:

S M T W T F S

GOD, WHAT ARE TODAY'S PRIORITIES?

○ _____
○ _____
○ _____
○ _____
○ _____
○ _____
○ _____

GOD, WHO DO YOU SAY I AM?

VERSE OF THE WEEK:

MEETINGS:

○ _____
○ _____
○ _____
○ _____
○ _____

TODAY I AM GRATEFUL FOR:

Daily PRAYER & RECONNECTION

DATE:

S M T W T F S

TODAY I FEEL

WHAT/WHO ARE YOU PRAYING FOR?

○ _____
○ _____
○ _____
○ _____

WHAT IS GOD SAYING?

WHAT IS MY ACTION STEP?

MY DECLARATIONS FOR TODAY:

○ _____
○ _____
○ _____
○ _____

ACTIVATE & DESCRIBE YOUR SENSES

WHAT THOUGHTS ARE COMING TO ME?

DATE:

S M T W T F S

Daily Questions & Reflections

HOW DOES GOD SPEAK TO ME?

WHAT IS GOD SAYING?

GOD, WHO AM I?

Daily PLANNER

DATE:

S M T W T F S

GOD, WHAT ARE TODAY'S PRIORITIES?

○ _____
○ _____
○ _____
○ _____
○ _____
○ _____
○ _____

GOD, WHO DO YOU SAY I AM?

VERSE OF THE WEEK:

MEETINGS:

○ _____
○ _____
○ _____
○ _____
○ _____

TODAY I AM GRATEFUL FOR:

Daily PRAYER & RECONNECTION

DATE:

S M T W T F S

TODAY I FEEL

😊 🙂 😐 🙁 😢

WHAT/WHO ARE YOU PRAYING FOR?

○ _____
○ _____
○ _____
○ _____

WHAT IS MY ACTION STEP?

WHAT IS GOD SAYING?

MY DECLARATIONS FOR TODAY:

○ _____
○ _____
○ _____
○ _____

ACTIVATE & DESCRIBE YOUR SENSES

WHAT THOUGHTS ARE COMING TO ME?

DATE:

S M T W T F S

Daily QUESTIONS & REFLECTIONS

HOW DOES GOD SPEAK TO ME?

WHAT IS GOD SAYING?

GOD, WHO AM I?

Daily PLANNER

DATE:

S M T W T F S

GOD, WHAT ARE TODAY'S PRIORITIES?

○ _____
○ _____
○ _____
○ _____
○ _____
○ _____
○ _____

GOD, WHO DO YOU SAY I AM?

VERSE OF THE WEEK:

MEETINGS:

○ _____
○ _____
○ _____
○ _____
○ _____

TODAY I AM GRATEFUL FOR:

Daily PRAYER & RECONNECTION

DATE:

S M T W T F S

TODAY I FEEL

WHAT/WHO ARE YOU PRAYING FOR?

○ _____
○ _____
○ _____
○ _____

WHAT IS MY ACTION STEP?

WHAT IS GOD SAYING?

MY DECLARATIONS FOR TODAY:

○ _____
○ _____
○ _____
○ _____

ACTIVATE & DESCRIBE YOUR SENSES

WHAT THOUGHTS ARE COMING TO ME?

DATE:

S M T W T F S

Daily QUESTIONS & REFLECTIONS

HOW DOES GOD SPEAK TO ME?

WHAT IS GOD SAYING?

GOD, WHO AM I?

Daily PLANNER

DATE:

S M T W T F S

GOD, WHAT ARE TODAY'S PRIORITIES?
- ○ _____
- ○ _____
- ○ _____
- ○ _____
- ○ _____
- ○ _____
- ○ _____

GOD, WHO DO YOU SAY I AM?

VERSE OF THE WEEK:

MEETINGS:
- ○ _____
- ○ _____
- ○ _____
- ○ _____
- ○ _____

TODAY I AM GRATEFUL FOR:

Daily PRAYER & RECONNECTION

DATE:

S M T W T F S

TODAY I FEEL

WHAT/WHO ARE YOU PRAYING FOR?

- _____
- _____
- _____
- _____

WHAT IS GOD SAYING?

WHAT IS MY ACTION STEP?

MY DECLARATIONS FOR TODAY:

- _____
- _____
- _____
- _____

ACTIVATE & DESCRIBE YOUR SENSES

WHAT THOUGHTS ARE COMING TO ME?

DATE:

S M T W T F S

Daily Questions & Reflections

HOW DOES GOD SPEAK TO ME?

WHAT IS GOD SAYING?

GOD, WHO AM I?

Daily PLANNER

DATE:

S M T W T F S

GOD, WHAT ARE TODAY'S PRIORITIES?

- ○ _____
- ○ _____
- ○ _____
- ○ _____
- ○ _____
- ○ _____
- ○ _____

GOD, WHO DO YOU SAY I AM?

VERSE OF THE WEEK:

MEETINGS:

- ○ _____
- ○ _____
- ○ _____
- ○ _____
- ○ _____

TODAY I AM GRATEFUL FOR:

Daily PRAYER & RECONNECTION

DATE:

S M T W T F S

TODAY I FEEL

😊 🙂 😐 🙁 😢

WHAT/WHO ARE YOU PRAYING FOR?
○ _____
○ _____
○ _____
○ _____

WHAT IS MY ACTION STEP?

WHAT IS GOD SAYING?

MY DECLARATIONS FOR TODAY:
○ _____
○ _____
○ _____
○ _____

ACTIVATE & DESCRIBE YOUR SENSES

WHAT THOUGHTS ARE COMING TO ME?

DATE:

S M T W T F S

Daily Questions & Reflections

HOW DOES GOD SPEAK TO ME?

WHAT IS GOD SAYING?

GOD, WHO AM I?

Daily PLANNER

DATE:

S M T W T F S

GOD, WHAT ARE TODAY'S PRIORITIES?

○ _____
○ _____
○ _____
○ _____
○ _____
○ _____
○ _____

GOD, WHO DO YOU SAY I AM?

VERSE OF THE WEEK:

MEETINGS:

○ _____
○ _____
○ _____
○ _____
○ _____

TODAY I AM GRATEFUL FOR:

Daily PRAYER & RECONNECTION

DATE:

S M T W T F S

TODAY I FEEL

😊 🙂 😐 🙁 😢

WHAT/WHO ARE YOU PRAYING FOR?

○ _____
○ _____
○ _____
○ _____

WHAT IS MY ACTION STEP?

WHAT IS GOD SAYING?

MY DECLARATIONS FOR TODAY:

○ _____
○ _____
○ _____
○ _____

ACTIVATE & DESCRIBE YOUR SENSES

WHAT THOUGHTS ARE COMING TO ME?

DATE:

S M T W T F S

Daily QUESTIONS & REFLECTIONS

HOW DOES GOD SPEAK TO ME?

WHAT IS GOD SAYING?

GOD, WHO AM I?

Monthly PLANNER

MONTH OF _____

SUNDAY	MONDAY	TUESDAY	WEDNESDAY	THURSDAY	FRIDAY	SATURDAY

GOALS:

CYCLE TRACKING:

TIPS & TRICKS:
- The best time for a facial is during the follicular phase of your cycle
- Add a simple daily routine of cleansing, toning, hydrating, and protecting your skin
- Enjoy a hydrating mask during the luteal phase of your cycle

Daily PLANNER

DATE:

S M T W T F S

GOD, WHAT ARE TODAY'S PRIORITIES?

○ _____
○ _____
○ _____
○ _____
○ _____
○ _____
○ _____

GOD, WHO DO YOU SAY I AM?

VERSE OF THE WEEK:

MEETINGS:

○ _____
○ _____
○ _____
○ _____
○ _____

TODAY I AM GRATEFUL FOR:

Daily PRAYER & RECONNECTION

DATE:

S M T W T F S

TODAY I FEEL

WHAT/WHO ARE YOU PRAYING FOR?

○ _____
○ _____
○ _____
○ _____

WHAT IS MY ACTION STEP?

WHAT IS GOD SAYING?

MY DECLARATIONS FOR TODAY:

○ _____
○ _____
○ _____
○ _____

ACTIVATE & DESCRIBE YOUR SENSES

WHAT THOUGHTS ARE COMING TO ME?

DATE:

S M T W T F S

Daily QUESTIONS & REFLECTIONS

HOW DOES GOD SPEAK TO ME?

WHAT IS GOD SAYING?

GOD, WHO AM I?

Daily PLANNER

DATE:

S M T W T F S

GOD, WHAT ARE TODAY'S PRIORITIES?

○ _____
○ _____
○ _____
○ _____
○ _____
○ _____
○ _____

GOD, WHO DO YOU SAY I AM?

VERSE OF THE WEEK:

MEETINGS:

○ _____
○ _____
○ _____
○ _____
○ _____

TODAY I AM GRATEFUL FOR:

Daily Prayer & Reconnection

DATE:

S M T W T F S

TODAY I FEEL

WHAT/WHO ARE YOU PRAYING FOR?

○ _____
○ _____
○ _____
○ _____

WHAT IS GOD SAYING?

WHAT IS MY ACTION STEP?

MY DECLARATIONS FOR TODAY:

○ _____
○ _____
○ _____
○ _____

ACTIVATE & DESCRIBE YOUR SENSES

WHAT THOUGHTS ARE COMING TO ME?

DATE:

S M T W T F S

Daily Questions & Reflections

HOW DOES GOD SPEAK TO ME?

WHAT IS GOD SAYING?

GOD, WHO AM I?

Daily PLANNER

DATE:

S M T W T F S

GOD, WHAT ARE TODAY'S PRIORITIES?

○ _____
○ _____
○ _____
○ _____
○ _____
○ _____
○ _____

GOD, WHO DO YOU SAY I AM?

VERSE OF THE WEEK:

MEETINGS:

○ _____
○ _____
○ _____
○ _____
○ _____

TODAY I AM GRATEFUL FOR:

Daily PRAYER & RECONNECTION

DATE:

S M T W T F S

TODAY I FEEL

WHAT/WHO ARE YOU PRAYING FOR?

○ _____
○ _____
○ _____
○ _____

WHAT IS GOD SAYING?

WHAT IS MY ACTION STEP?

MY DECLARATIONS FOR TODAY:

○ _____
○ _____
○ _____
○ _____

ACTIVATE & DESCRIBE YOUR SENSES

WHAT THOUGHTS ARE COMING TO ME?

DATE:

S M T W T F S

Daily QUESTIONS & REFLECTIONS

HOW DOES GOD SPEAK TO ME?

WHAT IS GOD SAYING?

GOD, WHO AM I?

Daily PLANNER

DATE:

S M T W T F S

GOD, WHAT ARE TODAY'S PRIORITIES?

○ _____
○ _____
○ _____
○ _____
○ _____
○ _____
○ _____

GOD, WHO DO YOU SAY I AM?

VERSE OF THE WEEK:

MEETINGS:

○ _____
○ _____
○ _____
○ _____
○ _____

TODAY I AM GRATEFUL FOR:

Daily Prayer & Reconnection

DATE:

S M T W T F S

TODAY I FEEL

WHAT/WHO ARE YOU PRAYING FOR?

- _____
- _____
- _____
- _____

WHAT IS GOD SAYING?

WHAT IS MY ACTION STEP?

MY DECLARATIONS FOR TODAY:

- _____
- _____
- _____
- _____

ACTIVATE & DESCRIBE YOUR SENSES

WHAT THOUGHTS ARE COMING TO ME?

DATE:

S M T W T F S

Daily Questions & Reflections

HOW DOES GOD SPEAK TO ME?

WHAT IS GOD SAYING?

GOD, WHO AM I?

Daily PLANNER

DATE:

S M T W T F S

GOD, WHAT ARE TODAY'S PRIORITIES?

○ _____
○ _____
○ _____
○ _____
○ _____
○ _____
○ _____

GOD, WHO DO YOU SAY I AM?

VERSE OF THE WEEK:

MEETINGS:

○ _____
○ _____
○ _____
○ _____
○ _____

TODAY I AM GRATEFUL FOR:

Daily Prayer & Reconnection

DATE:

S M T W T F S

TODAY I FEEL

WHAT/WHO ARE YOU PRAYING FOR?

○ _____
○ _____
○ _____
○ _____

WHAT IS GOD SAYING?

WHAT IS MY ACTION STEP?

MY DECLARATIONS FOR TODAY:

○ _____
○ _____
○ _____
○ _____

ACTIVATE & DESCRIBE YOUR SENSES

WHAT THOUGHTS ARE COMING TO ME?

DATE:

S M T W T F S

Daily QUESTIONS & REFLECTIONS

HOW DOES GOD SPEAK TO ME?

WHAT IS GOD SAYING?

GOD, WHO AM I?

Daily PLANNER

DATE:

S M T W T F S

GOD, WHAT ARE TODAY'S PRIORITIES?

○ _____
○ _____
○ _____
○ _____
○ _____
○ _____
○ _____

GOD, WHO DO YOU SAY I AM?

VERSE OF THE WEEK:

MEETINGS:

○ _____
○ _____
○ _____
○ _____
○ _____

TODAY I AM GRATEFUL FOR:

Daily PRAYER & RECONNECTION

DATE:

S M T W T F S

TODAY I FEEL

WHAT/WHO ARE YOU PRAYING FOR?

- _____
- _____
- _____
- _____

WHAT IS GOD SAYING?

WHAT IS MY ACTION STEP?

MY DECLARATIONS FOR TODAY:

- _____
- _____
- _____
- _____

ACTIVATE & DESCRIBE YOUR SENSES

WHAT THOUGHTS ARE COMING TO ME?

DATE:

S M T W T F S

Daily Questions & Reflections

HOW DOES GOD SPEAK TO ME?

WHAT IS GOD SAYING?

GOD, WHO AM I?

Daily PLANNER

DATE:

S M T W T F S

GOD, WHAT ARE TODAY'S PRIORITIES?

- _____
- _____
- _____
- _____
- _____
- _____
- _____

GOD, WHO DO YOU SAY I AM?

VERSE OF THE WEEK:

MEETINGS:

- _____
- _____
- _____
- _____
- _____

TODAY I AM GRATEFUL FOR:

Daily PRAYER & RECONNECTION

DATE:

S M T W T F S

TODAY I FEEL

WHAT/WHO ARE YOU PRAYING FOR?

○ _____
○ _____
○ _____
○ _____

WHAT IS GOD SAYING?

WHAT IS MY ACTION STEP?

MY DECLARATIONS FOR TODAY:

○ _____
○ _____
○ _____
○ _____

ACTIVATE & DESCRIBE YOUR SENSES

WHAT THOUGHTS ARE COMING TO ME?

DATE:

S M T W T F S

Daily QUESTIONS & REFLECTIONS

HOW DOES GOD SPEAK TO ME?

WHAT IS GOD SAYING?

GOD, WHO AM I?

Daily PLANNER

DATE:

S M T W T F S

GOD, WHAT ARE TODAY'S PRIORITIES?

○ _____
○ _____
○ _____
○ _____
○ _____
○ _____
○ _____

GOD, WHO DO YOU SAY I AM?

VERSE OF THE WEEK:

MEETINGS:

○ _____
○ _____
○ _____
○ _____
○ _____

TODAY I AM GRATEFUL FOR:

Daily PRAYER & RECONNECTION

DATE:

S M T W T F S

TODAY I FEEL

WHAT/WHO ARE YOU PRAYING FOR?
○ _____
○ _____
○ _____
○ _____

WHAT IS MY ACTION STEP?

WHAT IS GOD SAYING?

MY DECLARATIONS FOR TODAY:
○ _____
○ _____
○ _____
○ _____

ACTIVATE & DESCRIBE YOUR SENSES

WHAT THOUGHTS ARE COMING TO ME?

DATE:

S M T W T F S

Daily QUESTIONS & REFLECTIONS

HOW DOES GOD SPEAK TO ME?

WHAT IS GOD SAYING?

GOD, WHO AM I?

Daily PLANNER

DATE:

S M T W T F S

GOD, WHAT ARE TODAY'S PRIORITIES?
- _____
- _____
- _____
- _____
- _____
- _____
- _____

GOD, WHO DO YOU SAY I AM?

VERSE OF THE WEEK:

MEETINGS:
- _____
- _____
- _____
- _____
- _____

TODAY I AM GRATEFUL FOR:

Daily Prayer & Reconnection

DATE:

S M T W T F S

TODAY I FEEL

😊 🙂 😐 🙁 😢

WHAT/WHO ARE YOU PRAYING FOR?

○ _____
○ _____
○ _____
○ _____

WHAT IS MY ACTION STEP?

WHAT IS GOD SAYING?

MY DECLARATIONS FOR TODAY:

○ _____
○ _____
○ _____
○ _____

ACTIVATE & DESCRIBE YOUR SENSES

WHAT THOUGHTS ARE COMING TO ME?

DATE:

S M T W T F S

Daily QUESTIONS & REFLECTIONS

HOW DOES GOD SPEAK TO ME?

WHAT IS GOD SAYING?

GOD, WHO AM I?

Daily PLANNER

DATE:

S M T W T F S

GOD, WHAT ARE TODAY'S PRIORITIES?

○ _____
○ _____
○ _____
○ _____
○ _____
○ _____
○ _____

GOD, WHO DO YOU SAY I AM?

VERSE OF THE WEEK:

MEETINGS:

○ _____
○ _____
○ _____
○ _____
○ _____

TODAY I AM GRATEFUL FOR:

Daily PRAYER & RECONNECTION

DATE:

S M T W T F S

TODAY I FEEL

WHAT/WHO ARE YOU PRAYING FOR?

○ _____
○ _____
○ _____
○ _____

WHAT IS GOD SAYING?

WHAT IS MY ACTION STEP?

MY DECLARATIONS FOR TODAY:

○ _____
○ _____
○ _____
○ _____

ACTIVATE & DESCRIBE YOUR SENSES

WHAT THOUGHTS ARE COMING TO ME?

DATE:

S M T W T F S

Daily Questions & Reflections

HOW DOES GOD SPEAK TO ME?

WHAT IS GOD SAYING?

GOD, WHO AM I?

Daily PLANNER

DATE:

S M T W T F S

GOD, WHAT ARE TODAY'S PRIORITIES?

○ _____
○ _____
○ _____
○ _____
○ _____
○ _____
○ _____

GOD, WHO DO YOU SAY I AM?

VERSE OF THE WEEK:

MEETINGS:

○ _____
○ _____
○ _____
○ _____
○ _____

TODAY I AM GRATEFUL FOR:

Daily Prayer & Reconnection

DATE:

S M T W T F S

TODAY I FEEL

WHAT/WHO ARE YOU PRAYING FOR?

- _____
- _____
- _____
- _____

WHAT IS MY ACTION STEP?

WHAT IS GOD SAYING?

MY DECLARATIONS FOR TODAY:

- _____
- _____
- _____
- _____

ACTIVATE & DESCRIBE YOUR SENSES

WHAT THOUGHTS ARE COMING TO ME?

DATE:

S M T W T F S

Daily Questions & Reflections

HOW DOES GOD SPEAK TO ME?

WHAT IS GOD SAYING?

GOD, WHO AM I?

Daily PLANNER

DATE:

S M T W T F S

GOD, WHAT ARE TODAY'S PRIORITIES?

○ _____
○ _____
○ _____
○ _____
○ _____
○ _____
○ _____

GOD, WHO DO YOU SAY I AM?

VERSE OF THE WEEK:

MEETINGS:

○ _____
○ _____
○ _____
○ _____
○ _____

TODAY I AM GRATEFUL FOR:

Daily PRAYER & RECONNECTION

DATE:

S M T W T F S

TODAY I FEEL

WHAT/WHO ARE YOU PRAYING FOR?

○ _____
○ _____
○ _____
○ _____

WHAT IS MY ACTION STEP?

WHAT IS GOD SAYING?

MY DECLARATIONS FOR TODAY:

○ _____
○ _____
○ _____
○ _____

ACTIVATE & DESCRIBE YOUR SENSES

WHAT THOUGHTS ARE COMING TO ME?

DATE:

S M T W T F S

Daily Questions & Reflections

HOW DOES GOD SPEAK TO ME?

WHAT IS GOD SAYING?

GOD, WHO AM I?

Daily PLANNER

DATE:

S M T W T F S

GOD, WHAT ARE TODAY'S PRIORITIES?

○ _____
○ _____
○ _____
○ _____
○ _____
○ _____
○ _____

GOD, WHO DO YOU SAY I AM?

VERSE OF THE WEEK:

MEETINGS:

○ _____
○ _____
○ _____
○ _____
○ _____

TODAY I AM GRATEFUL FOR:

Daily Prayer & Reconnection

DATE:

S M T W T F S

TODAY I FEEL

WHAT/WHO ARE YOU PRAYING FOR?

○ _____
○ _____
○ _____
○ _____

WHAT IS GOD SAYING?

WHAT IS MY ACTION STEP?

MY DECLARATIONS FOR TODAY:

○ _____
○ _____
○ _____
○ _____

ACTIVATE & DESCRIBE YOUR SENSES

WHAT THOUGHTS ARE COMING TO ME?

DATE:

S M T W T F S

Daily QUESTIONS & REFLECTIONS

HOW DOES GOD SPEAK TO ME?

WHAT IS GOD SAYING?

GOD, WHO AM I?

Daily PLANNER

DATE:

S M T W T F S

GOD, WHAT ARE TODAY'S PRIORITIES?

○ _____
○ _____
○ _____
○ _____
○ _____
○ _____
○ _____

GOD, WHO DO YOU SAY I AM?

VERSE OF THE WEEK:

MEETINGS:

○ _____
○ _____
○ _____
○ _____
○ _____

TODAY I AM GRATEFUL FOR:

Daily Prayer & Reconnection

DATE:

S M T W T F S

TODAY I FEEL

WHAT/WHO ARE YOU PRAYING FOR?

- _____
- _____
- _____
- _____

WHAT IS GOD SAYING?

WHAT IS MY ACTION STEP?

MY DECLARATIONS FOR TODAY:

- _____
- _____
- _____
- _____

ACTIVATE & DESCRIBE YOUR SENSES

WHAT THOUGHTS ARE COMING TO ME?

DATE:

S M T W T F S

Daily Questions & Reflections

HOW DOES GOD SPEAK TO ME?

WHAT IS GOD SAYING?

GOD, WHO AM I?

Daily PLANNER

DATE:

S M T W T F S

GOD, WHAT ARE TODAY'S PRIORITIES?

○ _____
○ _____
○ _____
○ _____
○ _____
○ _____
○ _____

GOD, WHO DO YOU SAY I AM?

VERSE OF THE WEEK:

MEETINGS:

○ _____
○ _____
○ _____
○ _____
○ _____

TODAY I AM GRATEFUL FOR:

Daily PRAYER & RECONNECTION

DATE:

S M T W T F S

TODAY I FEEL

WHAT/WHO ARE YOU PRAYING FOR?

○ _____
○ _____
○ _____
○ _____

WHAT IS GOD SAYING?

WHAT IS MY ACTION STEP?

MY DECLARATIONS FOR TODAY:

○ _____
○ _____
○ _____
○ _____

ACTIVATE & DESCRIBE YOUR SENSES

WHAT THOUGHTS ARE COMING TO ME?

DATE:

S M T W T F S

Daily QUESTIONS & REFLECTIONS

HOW DOES GOD SPEAK TO ME?

WHAT IS GOD SAYING?

GOD, WHO AM I?

Daily PLANNER

DATE:

S M T W T F S

GOD, WHAT ARE TODAY'S PRIORITIES?

○ _____
○ _____
○ _____
○ _____
○ _____
○ _____
○ _____

GOD, WHO DO YOU SAY I AM?

VERSE OF THE WEEK:

MEETINGS:

○ _____
○ _____
○ _____
○ _____
○ _____

TODAY I AM GRATEFUL FOR:

Daily PRAYER & RECONNECTION

DATE:

S M T W T F S

TODAY I FEEL

WHAT/WHO ARE YOU PRAYING FOR?
- _____
- _____
- _____
- _____

WHAT IS MY ACTION STEP?

WHAT IS GOD SAYING?

MY DECLARATIONS FOR TODAY:
- _____
- _____
- _____
- _____

ACTIVATE & DESCRIBE YOUR SENSES

WHAT THOUGHTS ARE COMING TO ME?

DATE:

S M T W T F S

Daily Questions & Reflections

HOW DOES GOD SPEAK TO ME?

WHAT IS GOD SAYING?

GOD, WHO AM I?

Daily PLANNER

DATE:

S M T W T F S

GOD, WHAT ARE TODAY'S PRIORITIES?
- _____
- _____
- _____
- _____
- _____
- _____
- _____

GOD, WHO DO YOU SAY I AM?

VERSE OF THE WEEK:

MEETINGS:
- _____
- _____
- _____
- _____
- _____

TODAY I AM GRATEFUL FOR:

Daily PRAYER & RECONNECTION

DATE:

S M T W T F S

TODAY I FEEL

WHAT/WHO ARE YOU PRAYING FOR?

- _____
- _____
- _____
- _____

WHAT IS GOD SAYING?

WHAT IS MY ACTION STEP?

MY DECLARATIONS FOR TODAY:

- _____
- _____
- _____
- _____

ACTIVATE & DESCRIBE YOUR SENSES

WHAT THOUGHTS ARE COMING TO ME?

DATE:

S M T W T F S

Daily QUESTIONS & REFLECTIONS

HOW DOES GOD SPEAK TO ME?

WHAT IS GOD SAYING?

GOD, WHO AM I?

Daily PLANNER

DATE:

S M T W T F S

GOD, WHAT ARE TODAY'S PRIORITIES?

○ _____
○ _____
○ _____
○ _____
○ _____
○ _____
○ _____

GOD, WHO DO YOU SAY I AM?

VERSE OF THE WEEK:

MEETINGS:

○ _____
○ _____
○ _____
○ _____
○ _____

TODAY I AM GRATEFUL FOR:

Daily PRAYER & RECONNECTION

DATE:

S M T W T F S

TODAY I FEEL

WHAT/WHO ARE YOU PRAYING FOR?
- _____
- _____
- _____
- _____

WHAT IS MY ACTION STEP?

WHAT IS GOD SAYING?

MY DECLARATIONS FOR TODAY:
- _____
- _____
- _____
- _____

ACTIVATE & DESCRIBE YOUR SENSES

WHAT THOUGHTS ARE COMING TO ME?

DATE:

S M T W T F S

Daily Questions & Reflections

HOW DOES GOD SPEAK TO ME?

WHAT IS GOD SAYING?

GOD, WHO AM I?

Daily PLANNER

DATE:

S M T W T F S

GOD, WHAT ARE TODAY'S PRIORITIES?
- _____
- _____
- _____
- _____
- _____
- _____
- _____

GOD, WHO DO YOU SAY I AM?

VERSE OF THE WEEK:

MEETINGS:
- _____
- _____
- _____
- _____
- _____

TODAY I AM GRATEFUL FOR:

Daily PRAYER & RECONNECTION

DATE:

S M T W T F S

TODAY I FEEL

WHAT/WHO ARE YOU PRAYING FOR?

○ _____
○ _____
○ _____
○ _____

WHAT IS GOD SAYING?

WHAT IS MY ACTION STEP?

MY DECLARATIONS FOR TODAY:

○ _____
○ _____
○ _____
○ _____

ACTIVATE & DESCRIBE YOUR SENSES

WHAT THOUGHTS ARE COMING TO ME?

DATE:

S M T W T F S

Daily QUESTIONS & REFLECTIONS

HOW DOES GOD SPEAK TO ME?

WHAT IS GOD SAYING?

GOD, WHO AM I?

Daily PLANNER

DATE:

S M T W T F S

GOD, WHAT ARE TODAY'S PRIORITIES?

○ _____
○ _____
○ _____
○ _____
○ _____
○ _____
○ _____

GOD, WHO DO YOU SAY I AM?

VERSE OF THE WEEK:

MEETINGS:

○ _____
○ _____
○ _____
○ _____
○ _____

TODAY I AM GRATEFUL FOR:

Daily PRAYER & RECONNECTION

DATE:

S M T W T F S

TODAY I FEEL

WHAT/WHO ARE YOU PRAYING FOR?

○ _____
○ _____
○ _____
○ _____

WHAT IS GOD SAYING?

WHAT IS MY ACTION STEP?

MY DECLARATIONS FOR TODAY:

○ _____
○ _____
○ _____
○ _____

ACTIVATE & DESCRIBE YOUR SENSES

WHAT THOUGHTS ARE COMING TO ME?

DATE:

S M T W T F S

Daily QUESTIONS & REFLECTIONS

HOW DOES GOD SPEAK TO ME?

WHAT IS GOD SAYING?

GOD, WHO AM I?

Daily PLANNER

DATE:

S M T W T F S

GOD, WHAT ARE TODAY'S PRIORITIES?

- _____
- _____
- _____
- _____
- _____
- _____
- _____

GOD, WHO DO YOU SAY I AM?

VERSE OF THE WEEK:

MEETINGS:

- _____
- _____
- _____
- _____
- _____

TODAY I AM GRATEFUL FOR:

Daily PRAYER & RECONNECTION

DATE:

S M T W T F S

TODAY I FEEL

WHAT/WHO ARE YOU PRAYING FOR?

○ _____
○ _____
○ _____
○ _____

WHAT IS MY ACTION STEP?

WHAT IS GOD SAYING?

MY DECLARATIONS FOR TODAY:

○ _____
○ _____
○ _____
○ _____

ACTIVATE & DESCRIBE YOUR SENSES

WHAT THOUGHTS ARE COMING TO ME?

DATE:

S M T W T F S

Daily Questions & Reflections

HOW DOES GOD SPEAK TO ME?

WHAT IS GOD SAYING?

GOD, WHO AM I?

Daily PLANNER

DATE:

S M T W T F S

GOD, WHAT ARE TODAY'S PRIORITIES?

- _____
- _____
- _____
- _____
- _____
- _____
- _____

GOD, WHO DO YOU SAY I AM?

VERSE OF THE WEEK:

MEETINGS:

- _____
- _____
- _____
- _____
- _____

TODAY I AM GRATEFUL FOR:

Daily PRAYER & RECONNECTION

DATE:

S M T W T F S

TODAY I FEEL

WHAT/WHO ARE YOU PRAYING FOR?

○ _____
○ _____
○ _____
○ _____

WHAT IS MY ACTION STEP?

WHAT IS GOD SAYING?

MY DECLARATIONS FOR TODAY:

○ _____
○ _____
○ _____
○ _____

ACTIVATE & DESCRIBE YOUR SENSES

WHAT THOUGHTS ARE COMING TO ME?

DATE:

S M T W T F S

Daily QUESTIONS & REFLECTIONS

HOW DOES GOD SPEAK TO ME?

WHAT IS GOD SAYING?

GOD, WHO AM I?

Daily PLANNER

DATE:

S M T W T F S

GOD, WHAT ARE TODAY'S PRIORITIES?

- _____
- _____
- _____
- _____
- _____
- _____
- _____

GOD, WHO DO YOU SAY I AM?

VERSE OF THE WEEK:

MEETINGS:

- _____
- _____
- _____
- _____
- _____

TODAY I AM GRATEFUL FOR:

Daily Prayer & Reconnection

DATE:

S M T W T F S

TODAY I FEEL

WHAT/WHO ARE YOU PRAYING FOR?

- _____
- _____
- _____
- _____

WHAT IS GOD SAYING?

WHAT IS MY ACTION STEP?

MY DECLARATIONS FOR TODAY:

- _____
- _____
- _____
- _____

ACTIVATE & DESCRIBE YOUR SENSES

WHAT THOUGHTS ARE COMING TO ME?

DATE:

S M T W T F S

Daily QUESTIONS & REFLECTIONS

HOW DOES GOD SPEAK TO ME?

WHAT IS GOD SAYING?

GOD, WHO AM I?

Daily PLANNER

DATE:

S M T W T F S

GOD, WHAT ARE TODAY'S PRIORITIES?

- ☐ _____
- ☐ _____
- ☐ _____
- ☐ _____
- ☐ _____
- ☐ _____
- ☐ _____

GOD, WHO DO YOU SAY I AM?

VERSE OF THE WEEK:

MEETINGS:

- ☐ _____
- ☐ _____
- ☐ _____
- ☐ _____
- ☐ _____

TODAY I AM GRATEFUL FOR:

Daily PRAYER & RECONNECTION

DATE:

S M T W T F S

TODAY I FEEL

WHAT/WHO ARE YOU PRAYING FOR?

○ _____
○ _____
○ _____
○ _____

WHAT IS GOD SAYING?

WHAT IS MY ACTION STEP?

MY DECLARATIONS FOR TODAY:

○ _____
○ _____
○ _____
○ _____

ACTIVATE & DESCRIBE YOUR SENSES

WHAT THOUGHTS ARE COMING TO ME?

DATE:

S M T W T F S

Daily QUESTIONS & REFLECTIONS

HOW DOES GOD SPEAK TO ME?

WHAT IS GOD SAYING?

GOD, WHO AM I?

Daily PLANNER

DATE:

S M T W T F S

GOD, WHAT ARE TODAY'S PRIORITIES?

- _____
- _____
- _____
- _____
- _____
- _____
- _____

GOD, WHO DO YOU SAY I AM?

VERSE OF THE WEEK:

MEETINGS:

- _____
- _____
- _____
- _____
- _____

TODAY I AM GRATEFUL FOR:

Daily Prayer & Reconnection

DATE:

S M T W T F S

TODAY I FEEL

😊 🙂 😐 🙁 😢

WHAT/WHO ARE YOU PRAYING FOR?

○ _____
○ _____
○ _____
○ _____

WHAT IS MY ACTION STEP?

WHAT IS GOD SAYING?

MY DECLARATIONS FOR TODAY:

○ _____
○ _____
○ _____
○ _____

ACTIVATE & DESCRIBE YOUR SENSES

WHAT THOUGHTS ARE COMING TO ME?

DATE:

S M T W T F S

Daily QUESTIONS & REFLECTIONS

HOW DOES GOD SPEAK TO ME?

WHAT IS GOD SAYING?

GOD, WHO AM I?

Daily PLANNER

DATE:

S M T W T F S

GOD, WHAT ARE TODAY'S PRIORITIES?

○ _____
○ _____
○ _____
○ _____
○ _____
○ _____
○ _____

GOD, WHO DO YOU SAY I AM?

VERSE OF THE WEEK:

MEETINGS:

○ _____
○ _____
○ _____
○ _____
○ _____

TODAY I AM GRATEFUL FOR:

Daily Prayer & Reconnection

DATE:

S M T W T F S

TODAY I FEEL

WHAT/WHO ARE YOU PRAYING FOR?

○ _____
○ _____
○ _____
○ _____

WHAT IS MY ACTION STEP?

WHAT IS GOD SAYING?

MY DECLARATIONS FOR TODAY:

○ _____
○ _____
○ _____
○ _____

ACTIVATE & DESCRIBE YOUR SENSES

WHAT THOUGHTS ARE COMING TO ME?

DATE:

S M T W T F S

Daily QUESTIONS & REFLECTIONS

HOW DOES GOD SPEAK TO ME?

WHAT IS GOD SAYING?

GOD, WHO AM I?

Daily PLANNER

DATE:

S M T W T F S

GOD, WHAT ARE TODAY'S PRIORITIES?
- _____
- _____
- _____
- _____
- _____
- _____
- _____

GOD, WHO DO YOU SAY I AM?

VERSE OF THE WEEK:

MEETINGS:
- _____
- _____
- _____
- _____
- _____

TODAY I AM GRATEFUL FOR:

Daily Prayer & Reconnection

DATE:

S M T W T F S

TODAY I FEEL

WHAT/WHO ARE YOU PRAYING FOR?

- _____
- _____
- _____
- _____

WHAT IS MY ACTION STEP?

WHAT IS GOD SAYING?

MY DECLARATIONS FOR TODAY:

- _____
- _____
- _____
- _____

ACTIVATE & DESCRIBE YOUR SENSES

WHAT THOUGHTS ARE COMING TO ME?

DATE:

S M T W T F S

Daily QUESTIONS & REFLECTIONS

HOW DOES GOD SPEAK TO ME?

WHAT IS GOD SAYING?

GOD, WHO AM I?

Daily PLANNER

DATE:

S M T W T F S

GOD, WHAT ARE TODAY'S PRIORITIES?

○ _____
○ _____
○ _____
○ _____
○ _____
○ _____
○ _____

VERSE OF THE WEEK:

GOD, WHO DO YOU SAY I AM?

MEETINGS:

○ _____
○ _____
○ _____
○ _____
○ _____

TODAY I AM GRATEFUL FOR:

Daily Prayer & Reconnection

DATE:

S M T W T F S

TODAY I FEEL

WHAT/WHO ARE YOU PRAYING FOR?

- _____
- _____
- _____
- _____

WHAT IS MY ACTION STEP?

WHAT IS GOD SAYING?

MY DECLARATIONS FOR TODAY:

- _____
- _____
- _____
- _____

ACTIVATE & DESCRIBE YOUR SENSES

WHAT THOUGHTS ARE COMING TO ME?

DATE:

S M T W T F S

Daily Questions & Reflections

HOW DOES GOD SPEAK TO ME?

WHAT IS GOD SAYING?

GOD, WHO AM I?

Daily PLANNER

DATE:

S M T W T F S

GOD, WHAT ARE TODAY'S PRIORITIES?

○ _____
○ _____
○ _____
○ _____
○ _____
○ _____
○ _____

GOD, WHO DO YOU SAY I AM?

VERSE OF THE WEEK:

MEETINGS:

○ _____
○ _____
○ _____
○ _____
○ _____

TODAY I AM GRATEFUL FOR:

Daily Prayer & Reconnection

DATE:

S M T W T F S

TODAY I FEEL

😊 🙂 😐 🙁 😢

WHAT/WHO ARE YOU PRAYING FOR?

- _____
- _____
- _____
- _____

WHAT IS MY ACTION STEP?

WHAT IS GOD SAYING?

MY DECLARATIONS FOR TODAY:

- _____
- _____
- _____
- _____

ACTIVATE & DESCRIBE YOUR SENSES

WHAT THOUGHTS ARE COMING TO ME?

DATE:

S M T W T F S

Daily QUESTIONS & REFLECTIONS

HOW DOES GOD SPEAK TO ME?

WHAT IS GOD SAYING?

GOD, WHO AM I?

Daily PLANNER

DATE:

S M T W T F S

GOD, WHAT ARE TODAY'S PRIORITIES?

○ _____
○ _____
○ _____
○ _____
○ _____
○ _____
○ _____

GOD, WHO DO YOU SAY I AM?

VERSE OF THE WEEK:

MEETINGS:

○ _____
○ _____
○ _____
○ _____
○ _____

TODAY I AM GRATEFUL FOR:

Daily PRAYER & RECONNECTION

DATE:

S M T W T F S

TODAY I FEEL

WHAT/WHO ARE YOU PRAYING FOR?

○ _____
○ _____
○ _____
○ _____

WHAT IS MY ACTION STEP?

WHAT IS GOD SAYING?

MY DECLARATIONS FOR TODAY:

○ _____
○ _____
○ _____
○ _____

ACTIVATE & DESCRIBE YOUR SENSES

WHAT THOUGHTS ARE COMING TO ME?

DATE:

S M T W T F S

Daily Questions & Reflections

HOW DOES GOD SPEAK TO ME?

WHAT IS GOD SAYING?

GOD, WHO AM I?

Daily PLANNER

DATE:

S M T W T F S

GOD, WHAT ARE TODAY'S PRIORITIES?

- _____
- _____
- _____
- _____
- _____
- _____
- _____

GOD, WHO DO YOU SAY I AM?

VERSE OF THE WEEK:

MEETINGS:

- _____
- _____
- _____
- _____
- _____

TODAY I AM GRATEFUL FOR:

Daily PRAYER & RECONNECTION

DATE:

S M T W T F S

TODAY I FEEL

😊 🙂 😐 ☹️ 😢

WHAT/WHO ARE YOU PRAYING FOR?

○ _____
○ _____
○ _____
○ _____

WHAT IS MY ACTION STEP?

WHAT IS GOD SAYING?

MY DECLARATIONS FOR TODAY:

○ _____
○ _____
○ _____
○ _____

ACTIVATE & DESCRIBE YOUR SENSES

WHAT THOUGHTS ARE COMING TO ME?

DATE:

S M T W T F S

Daily Questions & Reflections

HOW DOES GOD SPEAK TO ME?

WHAT IS GOD SAYING?

GOD, WHO AM I?

 Scan the code, watch the video, and start your journey of connecting with God on a deeper level.

ABOUT THE AUTHOR

Hi! I'm Melissa Mendez, the face behind **Embracing Royal Beauty**. My life consists of many different roles, each filled with compassion and love.

As a daughter of God, I am honored to serve as a wife, homeschool mom, and entrepreneur.

Through my entrepreneurship, I support women with life coaching, esthetic services, and business consulting.

I am passionate about connecting with women to release divine strategies and solutions. Speaking wisdom into women and helping them discover treasures hidden within is a great honor.

I have committed to pursue a life of wholeness available through Jesus. My mission is to use my gifts to bring healing to families, from the inside out, through the hearts of women so they too can embrace their **ROYAL BEAUTY** and experience the fullness of God's Kingdom.

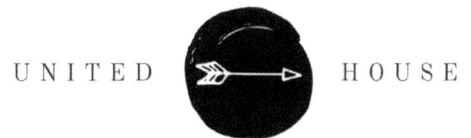

www.ingramcontent.com/pod-product-compliance
Lightning Source LLC
Chambersburg PA
CBHW051353110526
44592CB00024B/2971